Organizational Socialization

Organizational Socialization

Joining and Leaving Organizations

Michael W. Kramer

polity

First published in 2010 by Polity Press

Polity Press
65 Bridge Street
Cambridge CB2 1UR, UK

Polity Press
350 Main Street
Malden, MA 02148, USA

ISBN-13: 978-0-7456-4634-3
ISBN-13: 978-0-7456-4635-0(pb)

A catalogue record for this book is available from the British Library.

Typeset in 11 on 13 pt Sabon
by Servis Filmsetting Ltd, Stockport, Cheshire
Printed and bound by MPG Books Group, UK

The publisher has used its best endeavours to ensure that the URLs for external websites referred to in this book are correct and active at the time of going to press. However, the publisher has no responsibility for the websites and can make no guarantee that a site will remain live or that the content is or will remain appropriate.

Every effort has been made to trace all copyright holders, but if any have been inadvertently overlooked the publisher will be pleased to include any necessary credits in any subsequent reprint or edition.

For further information on Polity, visit our website: www.politybooks.com

To students

Contents

Tables

Preface

I have wanted to write an organizational socialization book for some time. I even outlined it years ago, but never started. When Andrea Drugan from Polity Press contacted me in January 2008, I was immediately intrigued. The timing was particularly opportune. I was scheduled to teach an undergraduate socialization class during Fall 2008 and a graduate socialization seminar during Spring 2009. The draft of the book would be due at the end of Summer 2009. That meant I could work through the book material twice during the semesters and still have the summer to refine it. I quickly agreed.

I want the book to provide both a practical and a scholarly understanding of the topic of organizational socialization. By attempting to do both, I may fail to satisfactorily accomplish either. I will trust the editors' experience with such matters.

Acknowledgements

It is difficult to acknowledge everyone who contributed to this book. Certainly, my Ph.D. advisor, Fred Jablin, contributed in many ways. His untimely death prevented him from continuing to influence this field of research. My students during 2008–9 contributed without knowing it through their discussions as I wrote outside of class. My adult children will recognize some of their work experiences as examples. My wife supported me as I accepted the project and throughout the writing. My parents encouraged me by asking for updates. They think that they might enjoy reading this book, unlike my previous one. If they do, it means that I accomplished my goal of being practical.

Like everything I accomplish professionally or personally, I see this book as further evidence of the blessings God has bestowed on me throughout my life. I am eternally grateful.

1

An Introduction to Socialization and Assimilation

After being hired during separate informal interviews, Marty and Pat, two college students, arrived at 7.00 a.m. Monday morning for their first day as part-time employees at the local chain restaurant known for its breakfast-type meals served throughout the day. They were immediately met by Chris, the supervisor who interviewed them. Chris informed them that they must purchase company aprons for the job and that the cost ($8) would be deducted from their first paycheck. They received a brief orientation and walkthrough showing them the dining area and the workstations, including where to pick up food orders. Then Chris assigned them each to shadow an experienced employee for the rest of the shift to teach them "how we do things around here." The six hours went by a bit slowly for the two "newbies" as everyone called them. After a slow breakfast run, much of the morning was spent doing side work, such as wrapping silverware in napkins. The lunch run was also slow with few tips. By asking questions of their mentors and observing the work environment, Marty and Pat began to catch on to some of the routines and learned some of the shortcut language. Their only interaction with Chris occurred at the end of their shift when they were asked "How did your first day go?" They both said it went smoothly and Chris replied, "I'll see you tomorrow."

Tuesday morning, Marty showed up for work, but Pat was a no-show. In fact, Pat never even returned to pick up the small paycheck for the six hours of work at the minimum allowed for employees who work primarily for tips. Chris told Marty, "I'm not surprised Pat didn't return. A lot of college students don't like the early morning hours and quit, although they usually at least give me notice."

Marty continued working for the restaurant for three years while attending college and eventually was promoted to shift trainer and then supervisor. The flexible hours adapted well to a class schedule that changed each semester, and allowed for vacation breaks. The tips made up for the low pay especially after Marty learned some tricks for increasing them, like schmoozing with customers and making suggestions that increased the size and cost of the orders. Marty even turned down a promotion to assistant manager because it actually meant more responsibility and lower pay with the loss of tips.

Pat did not mind the early morning hours like Chris assumed. It just didn't make sense to continue this new job when there was more money to be made by returning to work at the curbside-delivery, fast-food restaurant. It paid more than the minimum wage and, even though not everyone tipped, it was not unusual to make $12–15 an hour. Pat stayed in that job until an internship opportunity came up two years later. The internship paid less, but Pat thought the experience provided more career opportunities.

This hypothetical scenario briefly describes two very different organizational experiences. Pat and Marty began with quite similar experiences as they looked for part-time jobs and were hired after brief interviews. Their first-day experiences at work were quite similar on the surface: they had the same training and performed similar jobs. Their reactions to the experiences were quite different, however, and the result was that one quit after one day while the other became a valuable organizational employee for a number of years.

This book explores the experiences of individuals like Pat, Marty, and Chris as they seek out organizations to join, participate in them, and eventually leave them. This process, commonly known as socialization, is typically defined as "the process by which an individual acquires the social knowledge and skills necessary to assume an organizational role" (Van Maanen & Schein, 1979, p. 211) or the process by which employees are transformed from organizational outsiders to participating and effective members (Feldman, 1981). Using these definitions, it might seem that socialization only applies to Marty, who is the only one who successfully assumed an organizational role and was transformed from outsider to member. Since the terminology used in studying this phenomenon has been used inconsistently, some definitions are in order to clarify how all three individuals were involved in socialization processes.

Definitions

Jablin (1987, 2001) provides one comprehensive set of definitions for this area of study, although there are others. According to him, assimilation is the process by which individuals join, participate in, and leave organizations. Assimilation is further divided into two parts: socialization and individualization. Socialization is the process by which an organization attempts to influence and change individuals to meet its needs. Sometimes this socialization process is quite obvious. For example, in the scenario, when their mentors taught the newbies "how we do things around here," they expected that the newbies would adapt their behaviors to fit the organizational norms and rules. At other times socialization is more subtle, such as if Marty observed that most employees returned to work without taking their complete breaks and adopted the same behavior.

In contrast to socialization, individualization is the process by which individuals attempt to change organizations to meet their needs (Jablin, 2001). Hess (1993) suggests personalization as an alternative term for this activity. This term captures the idea that changes might range from something rather small, such as personalizing a work space with pictures, to something much larger like negotiating a different work schedule or position. Given the confusion that sometimes occurs between the terms individuation and individualization, personalization will be used here. Sometimes personalization is quite obvious. For example, as a valued employee, Marty was able to change schedules to fit vacations and semester schedules. Other times personalization is more subtle, such as if Marty has a particular way of organizing the side work. Of course, if other employees adopt Marty's approach, it becomes an example of socialization for other employees.

Socialization and personalization do not involve interactions between some nebulous organization and individuals. Instead they occur through communication between organizational members. Some of the more obvious attempts at socialization occur when established members attempt to influence new members. Personalization is common when established members negotiate changes in their situations with their supervisors. However, socialization and personalization are in constant tension with each other. Newcomers may enact personalization by demanding a certain work schedule in order to accept a job and established members may experience socialization attempts by other organizational members after being in a position for years.

Another way of describing the tension between socialization and personalization is to consider role negotiations in organizations as the interaction of role-taking and role-making (Katz & Kahn, 1978). Role-taking occurs when individuals adopt the role behaviors that are suggested by other organizational members – essentially socialization. Role-making occurs when individuals influence others to accept their concept of the role – essentially personalization. Since assimilation involves individuals developing organizational roles, these role negotiations are an ongoing, integral part of the process.

If scholars and practitioners used the previous definitions consistently, the socialization literature would be easier to integrate. Unfortunately, there are numerous variations on these definitions. Scholars frequently use the term socialization to refer to the overall process of individuals becoming organizational members, which Jablin terms assimilation. Perhaps the most contrary set

4

of definitions occurs in Moreland and Levine's (2001) study of groups. For them, socialization is the overall process of joining groups, Jablin's assimilation. The extent to which a group is able to alter the individual to meet their needs is an indication of assimilation, Jablin's socialization. The degree to which an individual is able to alter the group is an indication of accommodation, Jablin's individualization.

Given the variety of definitions used, it is imperative that readers of this literature recognize that scholars, the popular press, and the media use the terms inconsistently. For example, in the extreme, any *Star Trek Voyager* or *Star Trek Next Generation* fan might understand assimilation to be the complete take-over of an individual in which "resistance is futile." Assimilation into the fictional Borg society involves the complete loss of identity as individuals become robotic members of the society. The popular press makes little distinction between the terms, although socialization seems to be more commonly used. In this book, use of the term assimilation will be consistent with Jablin's definition, but the other terms, especially socialization, are used somewhat inconsistently given references to other research. Readers need to be flexible as they attempt to integrate the information.

Models of socialization/assimilation

A variety of somewhat similar organizational socialization/assimilation models have been proposed (e.g., Feldman, 1976, 1981; Jablin, 1987, 2001; Porter, Lawler, & Hackman, 1975; Van Maanen, 1975). The general merits of such models are discussed in the final chapter. Although they use different names to label time periods, most models have three phases in common. Most include a time period prior to joining an organization, known as anticipatory socialization or pre-arrival. This is followed by a time period of initial participation as a new member of the organization, typically called encounter or entry. The third time period represents the time when an individual is an active, established, or full organizational member, a period known as metamorphosis, role management, or change and acquisition. Jablin's (2001) model includes a fourth time period, disengagement or exit, to signify when individuals leave the organization. Similarly, the group socialization model has a remembrance phase for the time after an individual leaves the group (Moreland & Levine, 2001). A model based on volunteers follows a similar pattern of phases (Haski-Leventhal & Bargal, 2008), although it uses different terms for some phases (e.g., nominee for anticipatory, and retirement for exit). An adapted version of Jablin's model is used to organize this book: anticipatory socialization, encounter, metamorphosis/role management, and exit.

Anticipatory socialization

The period prior to joining an organization is called anticipatory socialization. During this time, individuals anticipate taking positions in one or more organizations. In the broadest sense, Marty and Pat were in the anticipatory socialization phase from the time they were born until they arrived at work that first Monday morning. It may seem inappropriate to view it this way, but by dividing anticipatory socialization into two subparts this makes more sense. Jablin (2001) divides anticipatory socialization into *vocational anticipatory socialization*, the process of selecting an occupation or career, and *organizational anticipatory socialization*, the process of selecting an organization to join. The former begins in early childhood as people ask children "What do you want to be when you grow up?" The latter is typically much briefer, lasting from the time individuals decide to look for organizations to participate in until they join them.

The term *vocational anticipatory socialization* has an implicit bias toward paid employment and suggests that the process ends when individuals enter their first career jobs. To avoid these preconceptions and include career changes and volunteer memberships, I use the term *role anticipatory socialization*. Role anticipatory socialization is the ongoing process of developing expectations for a role an individual wants to have in some organization. These role expectations are developed through interactions with family members and friends, educational experiences, other organizational experiences, and media portrayals of occupations (Jablin, 2001). For example, Marty and Pat apparently both anticipated a certain type of organizational role, that of part-time employees who were simultaneously attending college; neither saw their roles as long-term career choices. They likely anticipated other organizational roles not mentioned in the scenario. In addition to career roles after they graduated, they may anticipate roles as members of campus groups or volunteers in some community or religious organization. Chapter 2 explores more completely how experiences from childhood to retirement affect anticipatory role socialization.

Organizational anticipatory socialization generally occurs more quickly than role anticipatory socialization. Once individuals know the role they want to have in some organization, they go about selecting a particular organization in which to fill that role. Marty and Pat apparently learned enough about working at this particular restaurant to expect it to be a good place to enact their part-time employee roles; they accepted offers after the brief interviews apparently confirmed their expectations. If they anticipated roles in student organizations or local non-profit organizations, they likely looked for organizations in which to enact those roles as well. Chapter 3 explores more completely the processes that influence anticipatory organizational socialization.

Encounter

The encounter phase begins when an individual becomes an organizational member and assumes some organizational role. Regardless of the position or title, one component of that role is being a newcomer rather than an established organizational member. Being a newcomer is often an intense experience. Newcomers must learn the particulars of their organizational roles including understanding how to perform their jobs and relate to co-workers, as well as learning the organization's norms and culture (Ostroff & Kozlowski, 1992). In addition, they experience the interaction between their organizational expectations

7

developed during anticipatory socialization and the reality of their roles in the organizations (Louis, 1980). Marty and Pat have to learn their jobs as servers, how to interact with their co-workers and supervisors, and the organization's unique characteristics. Apparently the job seemed consistent with Marty's expectations but rather inconsistent with Pat's. If they joined student or community organizations, they would have similar concerns, learning their roles and determining whether their experiences met their expectations. Chapter 4 explores more completely the encounter phase experiences.

Metamorphosis / role management

Metamorphosis is usually used to describe a significant change in some phenomenon. In organizational assimilation, it refers to the change from being a newcomer to being an established organizational member. It is difficult to objectively determine when the encounter phase ends and metamorphosis begins. Although the encounter phase is typically thought of as the first weeks and months in an organization, time-based definitions are probably inappropriate for making this distinction. It is probably more appropriate to consider that transition from encounter to metamorphosis to be a psychological change that occurs when individuals no longer consider themselves newcomers. This may be a subtle transition in which newcomers switch from focusing on learning new roles to becoming comfortable and confident in them and feeling like established members (Schlossberg, 1981). In other instances, some meaningful event or action occurs, such as when newcomers feel like they have made important contributions to their organizations or more recent newcomers begin seeking information from them as veterans (Haski-Leventhal & Bargal, 2008). By quitting after one shift, Pat never experienced metamorphosis. Although it is impossible to tell when Marty became an established member, it likely happened around the time that newer employees sought Marty's help.

Although the metamorphosis phase can last from a few weeks to decades, it is not a stagnant phase as there is a continual interaction of socialization and personalization. By calling it role management, Feldman (1976) suggests that during this time individuals are both cooperative and innovative as they experience ongoing changes during their membership. Individuals become increasingly aware of the organization's culture, but, as it changes over time, they must adapt to it. Organizational members typically experience a variety of role transitions, either individually – such as when they change their individual roles through promotions (Kramer & Noland, 1999) – or collectively when the organization undergoes various changes, such as mergers or acquisitions (Zhu, May, & Rosenfeld, 2004). Marty experienced transitions by being promoted and by changing shifts during different semesters. It is easy to forget that established members, like Chris, manage their roles as they experience transitions, too. Established members must adapt to an ever-changing set of new employees and other organizational changes (Gallagher & Sias, 2009). Perhaps they must adjust to being purchased by another company. In addition to their work roles, Pat and Marty are members of their university and most likely various other organizations as well. As established members of those organizations, they experience changes in those roles as well. Chapters 5, 6, and 7 explore the metamorphosis / role management phase more completely. Chapter 5 focuses on the more macro experience of organizational culture. Chapter 6 centers on the experience of relationships within the organization. Chapter 7 examines transitions individuals experience as part of the ongoing changes and adaptations they make.

Exit

Organizational exit is an inevitable transition for all members as part of the assimilation process. Exit is typically divided into two types: (1) voluntary exit when individuals initiate the change, such as when Pat leaves after one shift or when Marty leaves after a few years; or (2) involuntary exit when others initiate the change, such as if a manager dismisses a restaurant employee for consistently arriving late (Bluedorn, 1978). Chapter 8 explores exit processes.

Theories for examining assimilation/socialization

Some scholars have referred to the socialization/assimilation process or models as theories (e.g., Feldman, 1981). In fact, they are simply heuristic models that describe a common phenomenon. Although focused theories explain particular portions of the process, many of the models are actually quite atheoretical. Much of the research is descriptive, consisting of typologies and explanations, but lacking any coherent theoretical perspective to explain the overall process. Although there are other possibilities, three theoretical perspectives have frequently been used to examine the overall socialization process: uncertainty management, sensemaking, and social exchange theory (Waldeck & Myers, 2008). A fourth one, social identity theory, has not been used as extensively, but has potential for making significant contributions to this line of research. Each theoretical lens provides unique insight into the process.

Uncertainty management

Various scholars describe the newcomer experience as one high in uncertainty. Newcomers experience uncertainty about their roles or jobs and how to perform them, as well as uncertainty about the organization's norms and culture, and how to relate to other organizational members (Morrison, 1995). Established members experience uncertainty as part of the assimilation process, as well (Gallagher & Sias, 2009). Marty and Pat experienced uncertainty about how to perform their job duties on the first day, but Chris also experienced uncertainty about whether these new employees would work out and how much supervision they needed. When Marty exited three years later, Chris experienced uncertainty about finding an adequate replacement.

Uncertainty reduction theory (URT) (Berger & Calabrese, 1975), originally an interpersonal communication theory, provides one theoretical framework for examining the assimilation process. URT originally included 7 axioms and 21 theorems concerning initial interactions between strangers. The theory's essence is that when individuals experience uncertainty about someone, that is, a lack of predictability, they seek information from that person to reduce their uncertainty. The premise behind this is that uncertainty is uncomfortable, and so individuals seek information to reduce it to reach a comfortable state. Accordingly, since Marty and Pat experienced uncertainty about their new jobs, they sought information, most likely from the people they job-shadowed on the first day, to reduce their uncertainty until they felt comfortable in their jobs. Similarly, Chris perhaps reduced uncertainty about the new employees by asking those same mentors about Marty and Pat.

A variety of important additions were made to the original theory. One of the most important of these was to recognize that there are different types of uncertainty. At one point, Berger (1979) distinguished between two types of uncertainty: (1) cognitive uncertainty, not being able to predict motives; and (2) behavioral uncertainty, not being unable to predict actions. Later, Berger and Bradac (1982) distinguished between three types of uncertainty: (1) descriptive uncertainty, being unable to identify an individual; (2) predictive uncertainty, being unable to predict an individual's behaviors; and (3) explanatory uncertainty, being unable to explain the reason for an individual's actions. Distinguishing between different types of uncertainty is important because it recognizes that individuals do not have to reduce all types of uncertainty in a situation to feel comfortable. They can manage their uncertainty in a situation by reducing some types of uncertainty but without needing to reduce all types of uncertainty. So, for example, Chris only needed to establish predictive certainty that Pat would not return.

Two important developments for URT were the recognitions that individuals do not always actively seek information to manage their uncertainty, and that they do not necessarily seek information from the source of the uncertainty. Berger (1979) found that individuals may use passive, active, or interactive strategies to manage their uncertainty. A passive strategy involves observing an individual to gain information. An active strategy involves requesting information from some person other than the source of uncertainty. Only the interactive strategy, directly communicating with the source of uncertainty, was conceptualized in the original development of URT, perhaps because it focused on initial interactions between strangers. In ongoing organizational settings, individuals have multiple information sources, from written or web-based materials to supervisors and peers. Marty and Pat likely used a combination of an interactive strategy, talking directly to others, and a passive strategy, observing others in the workplace, to reduce their uncertainty.

Kramer's (2004) theory of managing uncertainty (TMU) developed two more important points about how individuals manage uncertainty. First, TMU recognized that individuals often manage their uncertainty through cognitive processes rather than by seeking information. For example, by relying on past experiences, stereotypes, or imagined conversations, individuals create their own information for managing their uncertainty. Chris used cognitive processes, stereotypes of why college students do not like the job, to reduce explanatory uncertainty about Pat's failure to return on the second day. It mattered little to Chris that the explanation was not accurate.

The second important contribution of Kramer's (2004) TMU was the recognition that various competing motives may lessen the impact of uncertainty on individuals' behaviors. If uncertainty is the primary or singular motive, individuals are likely to seek information to manage their uncertainty. However, if individuals have other motives, such as impression management concerns or concerns about the social costs of seeking information, they may not seek information even though they are experiencing uncertainty. For example, Marty and Pat likely had a number of questions they could have asked Chris at the end of their first day to manage their uncertainty, but because they also wanted to make positive impressions as good employees, they said everything went smoothly instead.

Finally, managing uncertainty, rather than reducing it, has been the focus of more recent theories of uncertainty (e.g. Kramer, 2004). A focus on managing uncertainty recognizes that sometimes individuals even increase it instead of reducing it. For example, individuals with medical conditions sometimes avoid seeking information that would likely be a negative diagnosis in order to maintain uncertainty and hope (Brashers, Goldsmith, & Hsieh, 2002). In other situations, when a diagnosis is negative, individuals seek contradictory information in order to increase uncertainty and hope (Brashers, 2001). In the scenario, Chris may have avoided asking Marty about when the last day of work was going to be in order to maintain hope that Marty would not quit at graduation.

Uncertainty management provides an explanation of both the motives and the resulting behaviors individuals use to learn and adapt to their organizational roles during the socialization process. Further, it applies to all four phases as individuals manage the uncertainty they experience in selecting roles and organizations to join during anticipatory socialization, the uncertainty they experience as they learn their roles during the encounter phase, the uncertainty they experience during various transitions during metamorphosis, and finally the uncertainty they experience exiting. In addition, uncertainty management applies not only to individuals moving into or out of organizational roles, such as Marty and Pat, but also to relatively established organizational members, such as Chris. These individuals also must manage uncertainty about the changing members and their roles as they experience the ever-changing organizational environment.

Sense-making

Sense-making provides an alternative theoretical perspective for examining the assimilation process. Although sense-making as developed by Weick (1995) is similar to uncertainty management, there are some differences. Like uncertainty management, sense-making is concerned with how individuals understand or assign meaning to experiences. They differ somewhat in terms of how they view the process of assigning meaning.

Whereas uncertainty management generally involves seeking information to create predictability in a situation, sense-making generally involves retrospectively creating meaning to understand

13

experiences (Weick, 1995). So while uncertainty management typically involves seeking information to fill a void, sense-making typically involves assigning meaning to something that has already occurred. For example, Chris is involved in sense-making by retrospectively creating meaning for Pat's absence, in this case by relying on previous experiences with college students to explain the absence as a typical response to early morning work hours.

Sense-making is not an individual process, but rather an interactive, intersubjective process in which individuals create agreed-upon meanings for experiences through communication (Weick, 1995). Due to interdependence in most settings, individuals cannot simply create any meaning they like. Rather they negotiate an agreed-upon, intersubjective meaning through their communication. In this instance, Chris and Marty interact to create an agreed-upon interpretation of Pat's absence. Chris does most of the sense-giving by influencing Marty to accept the explanation provided (Gioia & Chittipeddi, 1991). If Marty had information about Pat's real motive for quitting and they discussed this, they most likely would have created a different intersubjective meaning.

Sense-making is driven by plausibility rather than accuracy (Weick, 1995). Ideally, individuals assign meanings that accurately represent the motives and actions of others. However, individuals can be quite satisfied with assigned meanings that are inaccurate. For example, Chris and Marty created an agreed-upon meaning that Pat's absence was evidence of an unwillingness to work early morning hours. Although a plausible explanation, it was not accurate. For Pat, pay, not the hours, was the reason for quitting. However, due to a failure to seek additional information, Chris and Marty assign an inaccurate meaning.

Finally, sense-making involves creating an identity (Weick, 1995). By making a commitment to particular interpretations, individuals create an identity (Weick, 2001). As individuals assign meaning to their past experience, they begin to recognize their own identity in relationship to the world they attempt to understand. Based on the sense-making that occurs, Marty begins to develop an identity as a good employee almost immediately, and

14

apparently kept that identity until exiting the organization three years later. Similarly, Chris's competence is reaffirmed by reiterating that it did not seem like Pat would work out from the start.

Sense-making provides another useful theoretical lens for examining how individuals assign meaning to their experiences during the assimilation process. It provides a way to understand all four phases, from how individuals understand their reasons for selecting occupations or roles in particular organizations during anticipatory socialization, to assigning meaning to their experiences as newcomers during the encounter phase, to comprehending their ongoing, ever-changing experiences during metamorphosis, and eventually to retrospectively making sense of their entire organizational experience after they exit. Due to its focus on the interactive and intersubjective nature of sense-making, it focuses attention on the communication that leads to the creation of meaning for both the individuals joining and leaving organizations, and those relatively stable members who must make sense of the changing organizational experiences.

Social exchange theory

Social exchange theory (SET) is the third theory that is very applicable to the assimilation process. SET is a generalized name used to merge the work of a number of scholars who focus on the way individuals weigh costs and benefits in making decisions about continuing or discontinuing social interactions. It is frequently criticized for being a very economic model for explaining human interaction, and yet it provides valuable insight into the assimilation process.

Thibaut and Kelley (1959) provided one of the most common explications of SET. The theory's essence is that people calculate how much effort or cost it takes to maintain a particular social relationship with an individual, group, or organization and the benefits gained from that relationship. Organizational members engage in both economic exchanges in which the exchange rate and transaction time are specified, perhaps in a written contract, and social exchanges in which the exchange is less specified, such as doing a favor for someone with no precise negotiation of what will be received in return or when (Roloff, 1981). At a minimum, individuals can exchange money, goods, services, information, status, and affect (or affiliation) (Foa & Foa, 1980). If the benefits equal or exceed the cost, the individual likely continues the relationship; if the costs outweigh the benefits, the individual likely discontinues it. As employees, Pat, Marty, and Chris all expect to receive paychecks in exchange for their continuing labor.

Thibaut and Kelley (1959) recognized that social exchanges are not simple one-to-one ratios and so explicated two different comparisons that influence cost-benefit ratios. First, there is the *comparison level* which is a fairly straightforward comparison of costs to benefits. These ratios vary according to the expectations for exchanges in particular settings. So individuals might expect that it would take several hours of service to receive a particular amount of money in one setting, perhaps a for-profit business, but expect a different benefit in a different setting like a non-profit organization. So, for example, even though Pat expects a certain financial exchange at the curbside restaurant of so much service for so much income, at the internship the comparison level is different since a certain amount of service results in less money, but more status (experience).

Second, there is a *comparison level of alternatives*. For this, individuals consider not only the comparison level of a certain exchange, but also the exchange ratios of other available exchanges. Due to this, an individual may remain in an unfavorable exchange because there do not appear to be any better alternative exchanges available. So an individual may stay in a particular job that is not providing a positive exchange ratio in salary because the individual believes that there are no other better exchanges available or that other available options, unemployment or working at a fast-food restaurant, are even worse than the current job. The comparison level of alternatives explains why an individual who is quite satisfied in a current job, say as a radio personality, accepts an unsolicited offer from a new organization because it offers a more positive exchange ratio through higher pay and a larger audience. Pat quits the job at the restaurant to return to a previous job because the comparison level of alternatives is more favorable in the previous job – more money for the same amount of effort.

Social exchanges are indefinite at times, with the exact nature and timing of the exchange quite open (Roloff, 1981). Individuals may provide a favor (service) and friendship (affect) to someone without expecting that these be returned immediately. They may repeat these behaviors without expecting repayment any time soon. For example, established employees may assist newcomers with information and labor for some time without the expectation that newcomers adequately reciprocate in the near future; appreciation (affect) may not be sufficient repayment in the long term, but sufficient in the short term. Of course, when an individual is no longer a newcomer, if he or she continues to expect assistance, but provides none in return, established employees may evaluate the social exchange as inequitable and no longer provide assistance.

This last example clarifies how relationships develop or fail to develop through social exchange processes. Communication is the symbolic process by which individuals provide or negotiate the exchange of resources, as well as discover and evaluate alternative exchanges (Roloff, 1981). When those exchanges are evaluated over time, and not necessarily in the moment, individuals determine whether to continue or discontinue the relationship, whether it is with an individual or with a larger entity such as an organization.

SET provides another important theoretical frame for examining the entire assimilation process. During anticipatory socialization, as individuals consider which roles to assume and which organizations to join, they gather information so that they can calculate cost-benefit ratios for the roles and organizations and make comparisons to alternative jobs and organizations as they make their decisions. During the encounter phase they communicate as they exchange services, information, and so forth to learn how to function in their jobs and organizations. They continue to communicate as they evaluate the costs and benefits of continuing their occupations during metamorphosis. Finally, at some point, the exchange seems unacceptable, either compared to the expected ratio or compared to alternatives, and they leave. So, for example, for many people, retirement at some point offers a better cost-benefit ratio than continuing working. In the scenario, Pat left after one day because the cost-benefit ratio of working at the restaurant was negative compared to alternatives. For Marty, the cost-benefit ratio was satisfactory until college graduation when other alternatives became more attractive. Chris apparently finds the cost-benefit ratio attractive or considers alternatives less desirable and continues to manage the restaurant. SET helps to explain how both individuals passing through an organization and those remaining in it for a long time make judgments about their continued participation.

Social identity theory

Although social identity theory (SIT) was not listed as one of the guiding theories used to examine assimilation (Waldeck & Myers, 2008), identity issues are explicitly part of the sense-making process (Weick, 1995). In addition, some scholars have called for examining identity as the central concept of assimilation (Forward & Scheerhorn, 1996). So, although there does not exist an extensive body of research on SIT and socialization, the existing research indicates that SIT likely provides a useful framework for studying socialization.

Ashforth and Mael (1989) articulate many of the essential tenets of SIT. According to SIT, the self-concepts of individuals are composed of two identities: (1) personal identities consisting of various individual attributes including physical features, abilities, cognitive and psychological characteristics, and interests; and (2) social identities based on perceptions of belonging to various groups, organizations, or societies. People tend to classify themselves and others in part due to associations with these collectives or social categories. When they identify with a collective, they may personally feel that the successes and failures of that group are their own and yet this does not mean that they have internalized all the values and attitudes of the group. They may also identify more with a subgroup, such as their work group, than with the larger organization. In addition, identification is more likely to occur when the group's values and practices are distinct, the group is perceived as important or prestigious, the outgroups are readily identifiable and salient, and the individuals share commonalities with other members.

This explication of SIT suggests that, of the three employees, Chris's social identity likely is more highly associated with the restaurant chain or at least with its local establishment. Pat probably never identified with either, and Marty possibly identified more with the role of server than with the organization. As part of identifying with it, Chris likely understands what makes the restaurant unique compared to other establishments, accepts many of its values, feels its successes and failures, and identifies with other long-term employees.

A number of important clarifications or additions have contributed to the understanding of SIT. First, as appealing as it may be to separate personal and social identities, it is likely that the two interact and influence each other so that this distinction is somewhat artificial (Alvesson, Ashcraft, & Thomas, 2008). Since some personal characteristics (such as race or occupation) are also group identifiers, it is difficult to distinguish between personal and social identities. For example, Chris's identity as a career restaurant manager combines personal and social identities.

Second, creating a personal identity is based in part on identification with particular organizations (ingroup) and in part on disassociation from others (outgroup) (C. R. Scott, 2007). In some cases – such as, perhaps, political affiliation – identification with one organization precludes identification with another, or disassociation from one organization leads to identification with another. In addition to identifying with the restaurant, Chris is likely quite conscious of the organization's competitors and perhaps even talks disparagingly about them.

Third, identity is not stagnant. Because individuals are simultaneously affiliated with multiple groups and organizations, they are constantly managing multiple identities (Cheney, 1991). Managing multiple identities involves increasing and decreasing various associations over time. As a result, identity work is an ongoing process in which an individual attempts to construct a coherent but distinctive identity (Alvesson et al., 2008). Individuals are constantly in the process of reproducing their identity or producing new ones by weighing particular organizational associations against others. So, for example, Marty's identity fluctuated over time depending on the level of identification with various roles, such as that of student, part-time restaurant employee, and any other roles.

The relationship of identification to commitment has been disputed by scholars. For example, some researchers believe that commitment should be considered one of the components of social identification or that the two are synonyms (Postmes, Tanis, & deWit, 2001). Others argue that commitment and identification are distinct constructs (Ashforth & Mael, 1989). Together, these arguments suggest that there is a high correlation between the two concepts, but that it is possible for individuals to strongly identify with an organization without being particularly committed to it, perhaps due to commitments to multiple roles. For example, Pat may identify with a campus Greek organization due to its values and traditions, but be unable to commit to participating in it due to work, school, and family commitments. Conversely, individuals may be strongly committed to an organization without identifying with it. For example, Marty may be committed to the restaurant due to co-worker friendships and its flexible schedule without identifying with what it produces or the values it espouses.

Overall, SIT provides another useful theoretical frame for examining socialization by suggesting that individuals consider how their organizational affiliations affect their identities throughout the process. During anticipatory socialization, they likely choose roles to fill and organizations to join based on the ease of identifying with them and conversely avoid others with which they cannot identify. Through a process of induction, training, and corporate education, the organizational representatives attempt to regulate employees' identities (Alvesson et al., 2008). As the newcomers learn about the organization's people and culture, they probably begin to identify more with the organization or a subunit and begin to internalize its values and practices (Ashforth & Mael, 1989). If or when they cannot identify with the organization or view identifying with an alternative organization or role more favorably, they likely consider leaving the organization. In the scenario, Pat apparently could not identify with working for lower wages at the restaurant and, as a result, returned to the curbside delivery restaurant. Working part-time at the restaurant was consistent with Marty's identity as a college student, but continuing to work there after graduation apparently was not. By contrast, Chris apparently identified sufficiently with the work as a supervisor at the restaurant to continue for years as a committed and loyal employee.

Evaluating the model and theories

The presentation of these four phases of the model suggests that individuals progress smoothly through them in linear progression. Jablin (2001) emphasized that the phases are more fluid. There is overlap between the phases and individuals may fluctuate back and forth between phases or repeat phases with the same organization (Feldman, 1981). In addition, while this model presents a generalized socialization process, socialization experiences are not the same for everyone. While some individuals move smoothly through the phases, others have quite different experiences. Some individuals may feel excluded and as a result never join or quickly leave. Due to factors that might include gender, race, ethnicity, sexual identity, physical abilities, and social class, some individuals are treated differently, have different access to information, and experience different stressors (Allen, 2000). As a result, they may always feel like "outsiders within" because they never become assimilated into organizational membership (Bullis & Stout, 2000).

Similarly, as valuable as these four theories are for studying the entire socialization process, each potentially also reinforces the illusion of common experiences for organizational members. Much like the model, each theory suggests that individuals have similar resources and experiences during the process. Each theory fails to explicitly recognize that, for a variety of reasons, individuals' experiences may be different. For example, when women enter predominantly male occupations or when individuals from a lower socio-economic status or a different cultural background enter predominantly upper-middle-class occupations, their experiences are frequently different from those of their peers (e.g. Dallimore, 2003). In terms of uncertainty management, individuals from outside the organization's dominant culture may be unaware of the information they should request or may not have access to sources of certain information due to their differences. Similarly, for sense-making, they may not have the previous experience needed to assign appropriate meanings to situations. In their social exchanges, their peers and supervisors may be unwilling to exchange information and support at the same rates as they would for others. These individuals may never achieve the levels of identification that SIT suggests are feasible. Along these lines, C. R. Scott (2007) suggests that, in addition to identification, SIT should be used to explore disidentification, ambivalent identification, and overidentification. Overall, this suggests that, when using these theories to explore the model, it is important to consider how the results may represent the experiences of many individuals, but also how the experiences of others might need alternative explanations. These issues are mentioned throughout the book, but especially in the final chapter.

Socialization and volunteers

Most research on socialization has focused on employment as the basis of organizational membership. For example, Jablin (2001) explicitly excludes volunteers from his summary of the assimilation literature and did not include them in developing his model. Such a bias toward employment is perhaps understandable given the economics of hiring and retaining employees. However, voluntary membership is a vital part of many individuals' lives, and volunteers are critical for the survival of many organizations. Over one-fourth of adults volunteer in at least one organization annually (Bureau of Labor Statistics, 2009). Volunteers contribute in excess of $150 billion annually in services to some 40,000 organizations in the United States (Fisher & Ackerman, 1998). These organizations provide vital goods and services to their communities that fill the gap left between government and for-profit organizations. Since these organizations tend to lose over one-third of their volunteers from year to year, recruitment and retention of volunteers is a critical issue (Corporation for National & Community Service, 2007). Given the frequency and importance of voluntary memberships, the socialization experiences of volunteers are specifically discussed in each chapter.

Conclusions

The socialization/assimilation process of joining, participating in, and exiting organizations affects everyone as organizational members, either through employment or voluntary associations. This process is typically viewed through time-based phases of anticipatory socialization prior to joining organizations; encounter during the first days, weeks, or months of membership; metamorphosis / role management when individuals feel they are full members; and exit as they leave. However, these phases are not as clear cut as the model suggests. Some individuals may feel like they never experience metamorphosis because they feel like outsiders during their entire organizational experience, even after years of formal membership. Others, like Pat, move quickly from anticipatory socialization to encounter to exit in a matter of days. Others may move in and out of membership repeatedly over a period of years, particularly if they are organizational volunteers.

Although various theoretical perspectives have been used to examine specific parts of the experience, four seem particularly valuable in examining the entire process. Each provides a somewhat different but useful perspective. Uncertainty management provides a lens for examining how individuals proactively seek information to create an acceptable or comfortable level of certainty or predictability in a setting. Sense-making focuses on how individuals retrospectively assign meaning to their experiences. Social exchange theory provides an explanatory framework for exploring decisions about maintaining organizational relationships throughout the process. Social identity theory emphasizes the way in which individuals come to identify with the organization through the socialization process. Together these theoretical perspectives provide a rich ground for examining the socialization process, although, by focusing on general socialization experiences, each potentially fails to recognize individuals' unique experiences. This book's remaining chapters build on this framework by examining these concepts and theoretical frames in depth.

2

Occupational and Role Anticipatory Socialization

Because math always came easily, TJ frequently tutored classmates who had trouble with their homework. Encouraged by teachers, TJ took the advanced placement math sequence that included calculus and the opportunity to earn six hours of college math credits before high school graduation. As a result, TJ became friends with classmates who took the same math sequence. Some of them, including TJ, even worked together part-time at a department store to save for college and have money to spend hanging out.

By graduation, most of the friends decided to attend the state university's main campus even though they were pursuing different majors. Teachers and family encouraged TJ to consider a math-related major like economics, finance, or accounting. They pointed out internet stories that said that individuals with accounting degrees received more job offers and higher salaries than most college graduates. In college, TJ found that economics was challenging, perhaps because it was not at all interesting, while the accounting classes were easy, but not inspiring. By focusing on doing well in accounting, TJ eventually received a number of offers by graduation.

TJ's father, who worked at an accounting firm his entire career, traveled a lot and missed many of TJ's school events. To travel less, TJ took a position in a regional bank's headquarters instead of the higher-paying accounting-firm job.

Learning the bank job took time, but TJ learned quickly and excelled in it, and received a promotion after just one year. Unfortunately, the work seemed mundane; it was difficult to see it was making a difference in people's lives. After discussing the idea with friends and family, TJ quit the bank job after four years to become a high school math teacher. The chance to meet a need for qualified math teachers mentioned in a newspaper article and to help students seemed like the opportunity to do the kind of satisfying work that TJ missed at the bank. Although TJ's father kept pointing out the lower salary and longer hours associated with teaching, the positive encouragement from other family members and friends to "find work you can be passionate about" convinced TJ that becoming a math teacher was the right decision.

Anticipatory socialization refers to the time period prior to joining an organization. Most individuals develop expectations beginning at a very young age about the kinds of experiences they will have when they join an organization. This anticipatory process is further divided into two subcategories. Role anticipatory socialization, the subject of this chapter, is the process of selecting a role, vocation, career, or job to perform in some organization. In the opening scenario, TJ first selected a role as an accountant and later as a math teacher. TJ also decided first to take a position in a bank and later in a specific school. The process of selecting a particular organization in which to perform a role, known as organizational anticipatory socialization, is the subject of the next chapter.

Sources of role anticipatory socialization

Communication related to five different sources is thought to have the most influence on individuals' role anticipatory socialization: family, education, peers, previous organizational experience, and the media (Jablin, 2001). Although they are presented separately in the following, the cumulative effect of these sources acting in conjunction with each other is more important than any one source.

Family

Attitudes toward work begin to develop at a very early age, influenced largely by parents although, with the changing make-up of families and extended families, other family members can be influential as well (Jablin, 2001). Household chores begin to socialize children concerning work. In summarizing research on children's household work, Goodnow (1988) reports important changes over the last 150 years. Children have gone from contributing to their family's economic welfare as workers on family farms or in family businesses to childhoods of leisure in which household chores, if any, are viewed as a way to teach responsibility and life skills. Whether or not allowance or pay is associated with these chores implies different types of social exchanges within the family that may influence future attitudes concerning compensation at work.

In addition, parents encourage general work and career attitudes by discussing general work responsibilities and providing work and career advice (Levine & Hoffner, 2006). Parents specifically encourage certain attitudes through the work narratives they tell their children (Langellier & Peterson, 2006). The work narratives often encourage children to believe in the dream that you can become anything you want to be, that you can pick yourself up by your bootstraps and become whatever you want, or that following the Protestant ethic of hard work will result in appropriate rewards. These narratives reinforce the rags-to-riches stories embodied in the popular works of author Horatio Algers at the turn of the twentieth century. Messages of self-reliance and unrestricted opportunity were prominent in the national narrative of the United States after the election of President Obama.

Family members often teach attitudes, skills, and behaviors that prepare children for various occupations. For example, factory workers attempted to instill specific work attitudes and behaviors in family members, such as working even when you are sick, for the good of the production line (Gibson & Papa, 2000). Workers wanted to be sure that they were not embarrassed by younger family members failing to maintain occupational norms. Of course, these values benefitted the organizations as much or more than the individuals and so should be viewed as socialization, not personalization. Similarly, parents in other occupations, whether they are doctors, computer analysts, or sales representatives reinforce attitudes and behaviors that may be advantageous skills or coping strategies if their children pursue similar careers.

Family members also encourage their children's pursuit of specific occupations. In some instances, parents encourage or even pressure children to pursue certain roles, either by following in the parents' footsteps to similar careers or pursuing some higher-status job. Parents serve as positive role models for occupations when they express satisfaction and enjoyment concerning their jobs. In other instances, families actively discourage children from assuming certain roles by emphasizing negative aspects of occupations. I am disappointed by the number of students who mention that their parents discouraged them from pursuing teaching careers because they perceive the pay as too low. Parents seem to provide more negative than positive messages about work (Levine & Hoffner, 2006). This suggests that family members may inadvertently disparage pursuit of certain occupations by talking negatively about their jobs without recognizing the influence this may have on their children.

Family members inadvertently socialize their children about work in other ways. Jablin (2001) notes that children often develop various strategies for avoiding work by the time they enter pre-school and learn which tasks they must complete themselves and which they can ask others to perform. Family members often perpetuate occupational stereotypes, such as when chores are divided along gender lines with girls doing more indoor cleaning and cooking while boys do outside activities like mowing lawns. Family narratives may imply that men should be the primary breadwinners and women should raise the children (Langellier & Peterson, 2006). With factors like location (rural or urban), parental status (married, divorced, single), parental education levels, and socio-economic class influencing these messages (Goodnow,

1988), parents are probably the most influential source of role anticipatory socialization (Levine & Hoffner, 2006).

The influence of family on role anticipatory socialization is apparent in TJ's occupational choices and work attitudes. Parental encouragement influenced TJ's decisions to take advanced math courses and pick a math-related college major. The fact that TJ's father traveled so much in his job at an accounting firm influenced TJ's decision to choose an accounting job at a bank instead. When TJ considered changing careers, the attitude expressed by family members to "find work you can be passionate about" supported the decision to change to a more satisfying career rather than one that paid the most money.

Education

Perhaps of similar importance to family, educational experiences provide additional role anticipatory socialization. Students learn about careers as part of classroom activities. For example, Jablin (1985) found that classroom books and discussions tended to over- or under-represent certain occupations compared to the general population. In addition, classroom activities seem to present certain communication styles as typical of certain occupations. For example, teachers and health care professionals were perceived as more responsive and receptive in their communication style than skilled/semi-skilled workers. In addition to these ambient messages about careers, many schools require students to investigate specific careers at some point.

Through their education, students learn about their interests and skills. Some learn that they are interested in and skilled at math and sciences, while others excel in the arts. Students try out possible occupations that involve physical skills, such as woodworking or cooking, as well as those involving primarily intellectual skills such as problem-solving or writing. As they near graduation from high school or college, students may use internships to experience occupations that interest them, whether in construction work or public relations. When their expectations are appropriate and they experience supportive socialization for the internship, they have more positive experiences as interns; this seems to affect their general attitude toward work more than attitudes toward specific vocations, perhaps due to the temporary nature of the internships (Feldman & Weitz, 1990).

Through education, students are socialized into the attitudes of chosen careers, particularly in programs that prepare students for specific occupations. For example, a longitudinal study of nursing students found that first-year nursing students learned basic skills and the ideal values and norms of their vocation, but that, during the following years, they developed more realistic views of their future careers and developed additional skills; they also became more confident and independent, attitudes necessary to succeed, while recognizing their need to continue to learn (Reutter, Field, & Campbell, 1997). Of course, this job-specific anticipatory socialization is not possible for many broad majors like psychology or communication which do not prepare individuals for specific occupations, but would be expected in majors such as accounting or journalism.

In addition to these specific occupational attitudes, the education system encourages certain general attitudes. Some of these are quite similar to those parents teach about the dreams of unlimited career opportunities and a work ethic. One of the most common attitudes reiterated in schools is the notion that "to get a good job you have to go to college" (Levine & Hoffner, 2006), a message repeated by educators with increasing intensity as students grow up. Increasingly, at the college level, the message is that to get a good job you need a Masters degree. While according to the 2000 US Census, individuals with college degrees make an average of $12,000 a year more than those without, since these figures include high-paying occupations like doctors and lawyers this hardly indicates that a college degree is necessary to get a high-paying job. The census indicates that only about 25 percent of the US population have at least a Bachelor's degree and only about 31 percent have college degrees, including associate or technical degrees. It seems rather elitist to imply that 70 percent of the population do not have "good jobs," and yet such an attitude is consistently perpetuated by the education system.

It is clear that experiences in the educational system influenced TJ's career choices, beginning with accepting that going to college was important for getting a good job. By being encouraged into the fast-track math sequence and finding some courses less interesting than others, TJ gradually decided on an accounting career and likely developed attitudes toward accuracy and ethics that reflected those of practicing accountants. But when that career was less than satisfying, the early experiences of enjoying tutoring other students influenced TJ's choice to pursue a career teaching math.

Peers

Peers are another important source of role anticipatory socialization although it appears that their messages tend to be more about negative rather than positive aspects of working (Levine & Hoffner, 2006). Peers influence attitudes toward work and occupational choices similarly to family members. Individuals learn about other occupations through interactions in which peers discuss their own or their family members' work experiences. It is not uncommon for high school friends to develop similar educational aspirations. Through this process, peers confirm or disconfirm the desirability of certain careers (e.g. G. W. Peterson & Peters, 1983).

Peer interactions during adolescence also may influence expectations for peer work relationships later in life (Jablin, 2001). Close friends confide in one another and develop trust. They perhaps keep secrets from those in authority, either parents or teachers. They practice communication skills working in classroom or extra-curricular groups or teams. Rival peer groups or competing teams often develop animosity toward one another. These various relational patterns may be mirrored in later organizational experiences with supervisors, peers in their own or other departments, or in inter-organizational interactions.

The discussion of peer influence on occupational choices has focused on individuals growing up. Peers continue to influence occupational choices later in life as they confirm or disconfirm previous choices or future career changes. For example, Tan (2008) found that individuals often consulted with peers as they considered changing careers later in life; they primarily discussed the decision with peers who they thought were likely to support their career changes. In fact, the individuals often consulted peers instead of family members, perhaps because they were considering downward career moves to ones of lower pay or status.

Overall, peers influence role anticipatory socialization throughout life. TJ's high school friends collectively assumed that they would go to college and confirmed that an accounting career was a good choice, a choice further supported by college friends. After finding the accounting job unsatisfying, TJ's peers encouraged pursuit of a second career in teaching. Since this topic is understudied (Jablin, 2001), the influence of peers, especially beyond initial career choices, deserves more attention.

Previous organizational experience

Jablin (1987) refers to the fourth information source as "part-time employment." This term shows bias toward individuals seeking their first career jobs after finishing their formal education. As such, it fails to recognize that individuals change careers frequently throughout their lives, that individuals may move back and forth between part-time and full-time employment, that individuals join organizations as volunteers, and that volunteer experiences may influence employment decisions. *Previous organizational experience*, the term used here, recognizes that experiences from voluntary associations and previous part-time and full-time employment all influence decisions to pursue various organizational roles.

Part-time work while in school is one part of these previous organizational experiences. National statistics in the United States indicate that 41 percent of freshmen, 65 percent of sophomores, 79 percent of juniors, and 87 percent of seniors attending high school work during the school year or the summer (United States Department of Labor, 2005). High school and college students often work in low-paying service jobs in the fast-food, restaurant, or retail sales areas. Very few students report learning job skills that transfer to later occupations or gaining information about career choices from these jobs (Levine & Hoffner, 2006). This likely represents a sample bias of students working to pay for leisure activities or college. For some students, these part-time jobs are entry positions into future careers.

Part-time work does provide opportunities to practice interpersonal skills that possibly transfer to other careers (Jablin, 2001). In their jobs, students learn how to communicate to manage conflict with peers, interact with those in authority, and provide appropriate customer service. Although this learning is frequently a trial-and-error process learned from positive and negative results, these same communication skills are needed in many organizational roles throughout life.

Participation in voluntary organizations also affects work attitudes (Jablin, 2001). By learning to work cooperatively in scouts or being encouraged to "give it all" for the team, individuals acquire the attitudes and efforts that are expected of them. Individuals learn to balance the needs to both cooperate and compete with others.

For some, previous work experience includes full-time work, in either temporary or career jobs. Accurate statistics for job and career changes are difficult to determine (Terkanian, 2006) but people tend to change jobs within five years of entering the workforce full-time and, unlike lifetime employment years ago, most people change jobs over a dozen times. In some instances, the changes are to similar jobs with perhaps better fringe benefits, improved work conditions, or a more desirable location that better fits the individuals' expectations or needs. During these transitions, previous experiences create occupational expectations for subsequent jobs.

In other instances, perhaps three of those job changes involve career changes, moving from one type of work to something dramatically different, perhaps from sales to research or from nursing to store management. In these cases, the previous experience most likely leads the person to change because the job was less than satisfying or fulfilling economically or psychologically, but those previous experiences still influence future occupational choices and expectations.

Although it seems unlikely that TJ's career choices were influenced by previous experiences in retail, other organizational experiences clearly played a part. The unsatisfying experience of working for the bank and the positive experience of tutoring in school led TJ to make a career change.

Media

The media influence role anticipatory socialization through the organizational roles and work attitudes they present. Although television likely is the most influential medium, other media contribute to anticipatory role socialization from an early age. For example, an examination of popular children's books by Ingersoll and Adams (1992) found that the books that depicted organizational roles promoted certain work attitudes and values. In particular, the children's books promoted technical rationality, a system of logical behavior that devalues feelings. In addition, they seemed to recommend not being disruptive by following organizational norms and rules, expecting work to be mundane or boring, and relying on higher-status individuals to solve problems. These attitudes suggest passive roles of fitting in rather than being assertive and proactive; they focus on allowing organizations to socialize individuals without encouraging people to personalize organizations. The characters also tended to reinforce sex-role stereotypes with men being adventurous and women doing unimportant work.

Books for adults, particularly self-help books, create role expectations that are quite similar to children's books although presented in more complex terms. Carlone's (2001) examination of advice books, especially Stephen Covey's 7 *Habits of Highly Effective People*, indicated that these books promote self-management and adapting to the organizations as the way to success. Rewards are connected to fitting into the organizational system. Again, this suggests that, rather than personalizing organizations to meet their needs, successful employees adapt and behave in ways that promote the organization's success.

Television also contributes to role anticipatory socialization. Television potentially introduces individuals to careers they may not have previously considered (Hoffner, Levine, & Toohey, 2008). In contrast to this positive effect, there are two general issues with the presentation of work. First, television programs over-represent certain occupations and under-represent most others (Signorielli & Kahlenberg, 2001). For example, the medical, legal, and law-enforcement professions are disproportionately over-represented compared to their percentages in the workforce. Alternatively, blue-collar work, farming, and many other careers are under-represented. The impact of glamorizing certain occupations in the media can be quite direct at times. The popularity of crime scene investigator programs since the late 1990s has led to a significant increase in applications to educational programs in this field despite no appreciable increase in jobs (R. Smith, 2007).

In addition to misrepresenting the frequency of occupations, the media also misrepresent the actual work (Signorielli & Kahlenberg, 2001). Based on media representations, lawyers rarely do research and spend most of their time in court, when in reality many lawyers never set foot in a courtroom. Police officers in the media routinely draw their weapons while capturing criminals and rarely deal with paperwork, while in reality they can go for years without drawing their weapons and spend hours on paperwork weekly. Although these examples are just a sample of misrepresentations, they demonstrate that the media over-glamorizes most jobs by focusing on their exciting and unusual parts while failing to represent the mundane aspects that all jobs have. At the same time, the media tend to present some occupations negatively: for example, business managers are generally presented negatively as incompetent, socially unskilled, or unethical and greedy (Lichter, Lichter, & Amundson, 1997). It is perhaps reassuring to note that few young people report learning about job requirements from the media (Levine & Hoffner, 2006).

The media likely contribute to young people's career aspirations. Hoffner, Levine, and Toohey (2008) found that, through a process defined as wishful identification, adolescents frequently reported career aspirations (dream jobs) that correlated with their favorite characters' occupations, educational levels, and incomes; however, work values, especially intrinsic values, were influenced more by parents than by television. Overall, media portrayals of occupations are unrealistic about most jobs (Jablin, 2001).

Because accounting jobs are under-represented in television programming, it might seem that the media would have no influence on TJ's career choice. However, in the opening scenario, the media influenced TJ's occupational choices. TJ's parents used media news stories to encourage pursing an accounting career, noting it was in high demand and paid high salaries. Later, the news story of school districts needing qualified math teachers helped to motivate TJ to change to a teaching career.

Outcomes of role anticipatory socialization

Communication experiences with family, educational institutions, peers, previous organizations, and the media combine to have a collective effect on individuals' role anticipatory socialization (Jablin, 2001). Based on these experiences, individuals develop expectations for roles they should pursue, as well as avoid. In addition, individuals develop attitudes about work, jobs, and volunteering.

Occupational values and attitudes

One outcome of role anticipatory socialization is that people in particular occupations tend to share similar values and attitudes (Feldman, 1981). For example, educators' values differ from those in medical professions. Even within broad fields, there are differences. Elementary school educators focus more on students learning while professors at universities are more likely to value research. Nurses' orientation toward patient care differs from doctors, even though both are in the medical field. These attitudes develop not only through the educational process, but also from communication with family, peers, and co-workers in previous jobs, and media portrayals. In broader fields of study which do not prepare for specific occupations, such as English or behavioral sciences, graduates share fewer attitudes and values and the influence of other sources is probably greater.

Occupational stereotypes

An unfortunate outcome of role anticipatory socialization is that certain occupational stereotypes may reduce the options individuals consider. Although there are other occupational stereotypes based on race and ethnicity, those based on sex or gender have received the most attention. In addition to evidence that family narratives and work assignments, along with children's literature, support certain occupational stereotypes, the media reinforce them as well. For example, research on television programs conducted by Nathanson, Wilson, McGee, and Sebastian (2002) found that there were more male than female main characters in prime-time shows. In addition, women more frequently had either no clear organizational occupations or stereotypical female occupations such as secretary, nurse, or teacher. Women tended to be more deferential, frail, emotional, and sensitive while men more often solved problems. This suggests the media continue to perpetuate occupational stereotypes for men and women, and also stereotypical behaviors within those roles; women are more caring, emotional, and social while men are more task- and action-oriented. Although there have been some gradual changes in these representations over the years, programs tend to reinforce stereotypes where "males are breadwinners" and "women stay at home" by portraying women as having to choose between high-status careers and marriage, even though over half the women in the workforce are married (Signorielli & Kahlenberg, 2001).

Another example of occupational stereotypes involves elected officials. Traditionally a male-dominated field, significantly more women hold elected office today than in previous decades (Cotter, Hermsen, & Vanneman, 2004). Despite these changes, even after Hillary Clinton's breakthrough campaign and Sarah Palin's nomination for vice president, there remains a bias toward men. Studies at Harvard (Institute of Politics, n.d.) and Rutgers (Center for American Women and Politics, 2009) indicate that the number of women in these roles has remained stagnant since the mid-1990s at about 20–25 percent representation in elected offices in the United States. Despite efforts to recruit women as candidates, most still prefer not to be candidates for major state or national offices. If this pattern continues, political office will likely continue to be perceived as a largely male occupation despite high-profile campaigns like those of Clinton and Palin.

Occupational stereotypes are part of role anticipatory socialization. For example, in a free-association exercise, college students associated a number of specific occupations with women (e.g., librarian, nurse, and social worker) or men (construction worker, paramedic); more generally, they associated women with "pink-collar" jobs and men with "blue-collar" jobs, although white-collar work seemed less gender-stereotyped (Glick, Wilk, & Perreault, 1995). This may explain why women have been more successful in entering white-collar jobs formerly dominated by men than blue-collar jobs. Data from the 2000 US Census confirm that some employment demographics reflect occupational stereotypes. For example, women still make up less than 10 percent of occupations like firefighters, truck drivers, electricians, and electrical engineers; men make up less than 10 percent of occupations like nurses, bank tellers, and secretaries (Cotter et al., 2004).

The degree to which people accept occupational stereotypes limits their choices. Qualified women who do not consider becoming engineers because they perceive it to be a male occupation or men who do not consider nursing because they perceive it to be a female occupation miss career opportunities because of their role anticipatory socialization. There probably was a time when accountants were mostly men, but now there is a balance in the field between men and women. Similarly, at this time, there are an abundance of male and female high school teachers. So, in the scenario, occupational stereotypes likely did not influence either of TJ's career choices.

Meaning of work

Perhaps one of the most important outcomes during role anticipatory socialization is an attitude about work and the meaning of work. An international research team examined people's work attitudes in a multinational study (MOW International Research Team, 1987). The researchers found that attitudes toward work varied along several dimensions: (1) How central is work to the person's identity? (2) How obligated does the person feel to contribute to society or some organization? (3) How entitled to work does the person feel (i.e., does society owe them the opportunity to work?)? (4) How important is it that the work expresses their personal values? (5) How important are economic compensations? (6) How important are different quality-of-work issues such as variety, autonomy, and responsibility? Based on a multinational sample, the meaning of work project identified eight main work attitudes (England & Whitely, 1990).

Apathetic workers do not see work as central to them and feel little obligation to contribute, are not concerned about work expressing their values, score relatively low on economic compensation, but feel entitled to work. They tend to be in low-paying jobs and dissatisfied. They value family, leisure, and interpersonal contacts more than work. *Alienated workers* are quite similar to apathetic workers, but feel a high obligation to work. They gain satisfaction more from family and religious activities. Their work is often repetitious and relatively low paying.

Economic workers feel entitled to work and value the money they receive rather than the opportunity to express their values. Despite concern over money, they tend to have limited education and lower-paying jobs. *High rights and duties economic workers* vary slightly from economic workers because they feel an obligation to work along with the entitlement to work. They focus on economic issues rather than expressing values through work. Perhaps because they tend to be older, they often receive above-average pay.

Techno-bureaucratic workers focus on quality of work and desire autonomy, responsibility, and a sense that their skills are being used. They are typically well-educated and receive average compensation and identify with their work. Their ratings of work centrality and expression of work values are at moderate or average levels compared to other types of workers. In contrast to others, for *duty-oriented social contribution workers* the ability to express their values is most important. Work is central to them and they feel a strong sense of obligation to their work. Economic concerns are limited although they receive average compensation. They tend to be well-educated workers who value autonomy, responsibility, and skill utilization.

For *work-centered expressive values workers*, work is central and expressing their values is more important than working out of obligation or for economic gain. They value work variety and autonomy and have the highest levels of work satisfaction and commitment. Finally, for *work-centered and balanced values workers*, work is central along with high opportunity to express values, but they are equally concerned about economic benefits. They are somewhat more motivated by obligation.

In examining this list, it is probably easy to think of people who fit most of the categories. The student working a part-time job for disposable income is likely an apathetic or economic worker. The dedicated teacher or social worker probably fits the duty-oriented, social contribution worker. Someone working in the fine arts or non-profit sector might be a work-centered expressive values worker.

It is important to consider the meaning of work as an important outcome of the anticipatory socialization process. Through their experiences, individuals develop their own meaning for work. Some of these worker types are more common in some countries than others. For example techno-bureaucratic workers are particularly common in the United States (England & Whitely, 1990). The meanings individuals develop impact their expectations for work. In addition, the work attitudes affect work behaviors after they join organizations (MOW International Research Team, 1987). For example, individuals for whom work is more central to their identity are more likely to work longer hours and be more committed to their jobs. Employees motivated by the ability to express their values will be less satisfied or motivated in higher-paying jobs that are repetitive and unrelated to their values than in lower-paying jobs that express them. So in addition to selecting roles or occupations during anticipatory socialization, individuals develop attitudes toward work. These attitudes change as work conditions and experiences continue throughout a lifetime.

From the few details provided, TJ may have started out as a techno-bureaucratic worker, a well-educated worker who desired responsibility and skill utilization in exchange for pay and status. TJ's bank accountant job had these characteristics. However, the meaning of work and the importance of work characteristics changed over time as satisfaction with the accountant job decreased. TJ eventually wanted an occupation that expressed the values of a duty-oriented social contribution worker who contributed to society by assisting others through teaching.

Perceptions of a real job

Another outcome of role anticipatory socialization is that individuals develop a sense of what is "a real job." In her seminal study of this concept, Clair (1996) examined college student essays describing what a real job meant to them. The most common characteristics of real jobs were that they involved money, utilized one's education, were enjoyable, involved a fairly standard work week, and provided opportunity for advancement in a reputable company. Something was "not a real job" if management was poorly organized and mistreated employees, or if it was voluntary, part-time, or seasonal work.

Individuals' ideas about a real job change over time (Clair, 1996). Young adolescents might perceive babysitting or delivering newspapers as real jobs because they involve pay outside the home, but later consider those not real jobs compared to working at a restaurant. If the individual graduates from college, a restaurant job might not be perceived as a real job compared to working full-time in a career occupation with health and retirement benefits.

The meaning of a real job is certainly subjective. College students' definitions show a bias against physical labor and toward white-collar-type jobs. Some individuals consider stay-at-home parenting a real job while others do not (Kramer & Walker, 1998). It seems likely that two individuals working side by side, one who considers their employment a real job and one who does not, have different work habits and attitudes. For example, TJ likely did not consider the job at the department store "a real job"; it was just temporary employment to make some money. TJ's co-workers or supervisors might have considered the same job real because it was their long-term, career occupation. TJ probably considered both the accounting and teaching jobs to be "real jobs." An individual's conception of a real job is the result of communication from family, education, peers, previous experience, and the media.

Perceptions of voluntary roles

Volunteer work does not appear to fit most individuals' conceptions of a real job, and yet many individuals spend a great deal of time "working" as volunteers. Members of non-profit organizations spend an average of 4.5 hours per week in these voluntary associations (Hooghe, 2003). Roles range from rather limited participation – such as occasionally donating money to charity or blood to the American Red Cross – to attending activities such as festivals, performances, or religious services, to active participation as planners and producers of those activities or in roles as officers who maintain the viability of the organizations.

Although research has generally not examined how role anticipatory socialization works for volunteers, it likely works very similarly to employment (Kramer, forthcoming). Family members either model and encourage participation in volunteer activities or suggest that they are unimportant. Educational experiences help to create attitudes toward volunteering as high school and college students participate in volunteer work such as tutoring or service learning programs with community groups. By supporting or making fun of volunteers, peers probably influence long-term attitudes about volunteering. The quality of the organizational experiences as volunteers – whether picking up trash as a scout, organizing a blood drive as a student, or rebuilding homes after a natural disaster as part of a mission trip – and the interpersonal relationships that develop during those activities no doubt influence the likelihood of volunteering in other organizations at a later date. Media portrayals of volunteers, as infrequently as they occur, do appear in news reports and occasionally in regular programming, for example when parents are involved in the parent–teacher association at their children's schools. Certainly, producers of public service announcements, such as "Be a Mentor," hope that they contribute to encouraging people to assume volunteer roles. No doubt there are stereotypes about people who volunteer in certain organizations. Together, communication from these sources leads to certain attitudes about the likelihood of assuming roles as volunteers and expectations for those roles.

Differences in Role Anticipatory Socialization

The preceding discussion suggests a number of powerful, but questionable assumptions about role anticipatory socialization. For example, messages from various sources that "you can be whatever you want" suggest that the dreams of unlimited career opportunities are available to everyone. Compelling stories of extraordinary individuals succeeding despite seemingly insurmountable odds keep this myth alive without recognizing the realities that many individuals face. For example, a Chicago elementary teacher once told me that some students had trouble completing an assignment to interview someone working full-time because no one on their block and none of their relatives held such jobs. Educational opportunities are not equal across districts, nor is there equal access to a college education.

Other messages seem indicative of certain socio-economic classes. The encouragement to "do something you are passionate about" may be plausible for TJ who is choosing between two well-paying, professional careers or for individuals in dual-career relationships. For an unemployed individual, perhaps supporting a family, income for survival takes precedence over passion for the job. Overall, it is important to recognize that, due to differences in background and context, individuals do not receive the same messages or have the same options during role anticipatory socialization.

Conclusions

The location of role anticipatory socialization in assimilation models might give the incorrect impression that it ends at some particular point. Due to the frequency with which individuals change jobs, change careers, and change voluntary associations, anticipatory socialization is a life-long experience. In the opening scenario, TJ continued to experience role anticipatory socialization after taking the accounting job. In fact, the additional work experience influenced TJ's decision to change occupations. Experiences throughout life with family, educational institutions, peers, organizational memberships, and the media continue to influence attitudes toward work, what constitutes a real job, and volunteering, throughout a life-time. Even in retirement, individuals continue to anticipate organizational roles they may assume. Some of these sources are more influential at certain times, and not everyone receives the same messages or perceives they have the same options, but, equipped with expectations for the types of roles to pursue, individuals determine which organizations to join to fulfill those roles. That process, organizational anticipatory socialization, is the topic of the next chapter.

3

Organizational Anticipatory Socialization

Even though they sat across the restaurant table from one another, Amari and Casey arrived through quite different paths. Amari learned about the job opportunities at Mid-US Insurance through the university placement office. The university brought in various company recruiters to assist seniors in their job searches. After researching on the World Wide Web, Amari decided to apply to Mid-US Insurance through the placement office, submitted a résumé, signed up for a screening interview, and arrived early at the assigned room. The interviewer started off talking briefly about the company. It seemed like several minutes passed before Amari got the opportunity to talk much. Some of the information was on the résumé, but Amari sensed that it was worth repeating because the interviewer may not have read it carefully. Gradually, the conversation became friendlier. They took turns discussing a range of topics like the company, their experiences, and the fact that they both lived in Chicago once. Except for the first couple of minutes, Amari felt the interview was more of a friendly conversation than the interrogations that characterized previous screening interviews. Amari seemed to have the needed qualifications and thought that the interview went well, and so was not surprised a few days later when the call came for the on-site interview at the company headquarters.

Casey's path to the lunch was quite different. After working for over a decade for a different insurance company, a friend who worked for Mid-US Insurance told Casey that the company was hiring. Casey did not do much research due to knowing the company as a competitor and simply sent a résumé and cover letter to the human resources department. After a brief phone interview with someone from Human Resources to verify some information on the résumé, there was another phone interview with a departmental supervisor that went very well and then came the request to come for this half-day interview.

Both Casey and Amari had a number of individual interviews during the morning with potential supervisors and peers, along with a joint briefing session from someone in HR who told them about the company benefit packages and policies that might influence their decision to join if they received offers. Lunch included an additional group of potential co-workers. The conversation included a lot of topics about work, but other topics as well. It came up that Casey was married and Amari was not. They both were sports fans although Casey preferred baseball and Amari basketball.

By the time they left, both Casey and Amari felt confident that they would receive offers. Eager for a post-graduation job, Amari was thrilled with the prospect of accepting a job with a company that provided so many opportunities and had good benefits. It might not be the ideal job, but it would be a good place to gain some experience. By contrast, Casey did not expect to accept the offer because it did not seem like Mid-US Insurance offered any real advantages, and the loss of seniority and retirement benefits did not make the prospect of an offer very appealing, unless the salary was substantially higher, but that did not seem likely based on the salary ranges mentioned. But Casey was still pleased with the opportunity to learn about other options and knew that having an offer might lead to a raise at work.

Along with deciding the roles individuals would like to assume in organizations comes the process of selecting organizations to join and taking the necessary steps to make that possible. The process of selecting an organization to join, known as organizational anticipatory socialization, is the focus of this chapter.

Comparing role and organizational anticipatory socialization

Organizational anticipatory socialization is different from role anticipatory socialization in a number of important ways. Role anticipatory socialization is a life-long process that affects occupational or role choices. Contrary to conceptualizations which present it as a pre-employment phase, it continues and influences decisions to maintain or change occupations throughout life. In addition, much of it occurs at a subconscious level as individuals gradually come to prefer certain roles over others and develop attitudes about work and jobs. Most individuals cannot pinpoint the day that they decided to pursue a certain occupation. By contrast, organizational anticipatory socialization is usually a rather short-term decision made quite consciously. People typically select an organization to join in a period of a few days or weeks, or in some cases a few months. Most individuals can remember when they decided to take a job in a particular organization or join one as a volunteer.

The fact that one decision is less conscious than the other does not indicate that one is necessarily a more rational decision. Typical models of rational decision-making suggest that individuals should identify the problem or issue, develop criteria for making a decision, consider various alternatives, weigh the advantages and disadvantages of each alternative, and then select the best option (Dewey, 1910). No doubt some individuals do this over time in selecting an occupation and/or in selecting an organization. Consistent with social exchange theory, they make decisions about careers and organizations based on a cost-benefit analysis. For example, an individual may gradually decide to pursue a nursing career because it offers better opportunities and salary for the same education compared to being a social worker, even though both careers seem desirable for other reasons like the ability to help others. An individual may take a job at one hospital because it provides more benefits and a more flexible work schedule, although the pay is the same. Other individuals likely based both decisions on something more intuitive or emotional, such as hunches or feelings. A person might pursue a career as a commercial artist because "it's what I like doing" and join a particular company because "it just felt right." The degree to which these decisions are rational or intuitive is probably more an individual difference that a difference between the two types of decisions.

Perhaps the most important difference between role and organizational anticipatory socialization is that choosing a career or role to pursue is very much an individual choice while choosing an organization in which to perform the role is a mutual choice. Individuals can choose to pursue almost any occupation if they are willing to gain the necessary knowledge and experience. This does not guarantee that they will find an organization in which to practice the role. An individual may want a job in a particular organization, but the choice must be mutual. Both the individual and the members of the organization must agree to the choice. For a variety of reasons, the organization may not ask an individual to join. There may be more qualified applicants or no openings. Likewise, the individual may not accept an offer after determining that the organization is not as desirable as first thought or learning of other more preferable options. Most research and popular press writing in this area is based on the notion that the mutual selection process is about finding a good person–job fit or person–organization fit (Jablin, 2001).

Finally, due to the mutual selection process, it is during organizational anticipatory socialization that the interaction begins between the organization's socialization attempts and the members' personalization attempts. Most scholarship on this part of the process is very descriptive and does not give any consideration of the interaction of these two processes.

Organizational anticipatory socialization involves two main activities. The first part of the recruitment process involves the interaction of organizations providing information to attract potential members (recruitment) with individuals seeking information as part of their efforts to find organizations to join (reconnaissance) (Moreland & Levine, 2001). The second part of the recruitment process is the actual selection process in which individuals and organizational representatives are involved in interviews in which decisions are made about whether individuals will join the organization. A third part of the process will also be briefly discussed. The pre-entry phase is the time between when an individual agrees to join an organization and then actually joins.

Part 1: Recruiting and reconnaissance

Because organizational anticipatory socialization involves a mutual selection process, organizations must recruit individuals. At the same time, individuals must seek out information about organizations to potentially join. Although recruitment and reconnaissance generally work together in a positive manner, at times they have conflicting goals and objectives.

Recruitment process

For the organization, the recruitment process involves three main steps. Research suggests that organizations improve their recruitment by focusing on recruitment objectives, recruitment strategies, and recruitment activities (Breaugh & Starke, 2000). First, organizations should develop clear recruitment objectives. These objectives go beyond "getting good applicants" to include consideration of the number and type of positions to be filled, and the diversity of applicants desired. These objectives influence the choice of strategies since recruiting diverse applicants necessarily involves different strategies from when simply seeking large numbers of candidates.

Once the objectives are known, a strategy can be developed to accomplish those goals. This involves selecting the appropriate recruitment sources for communicating the availability of positions to attract the desired recruits while considering the costs of the alternatives. Maintaining an application link on the webpage costs very little compared to campus visits or job fairs, but attracts different applicants. Selecting a strategy also involves determining the message content to include. When an organization is unfamiliar to most potential applicants, messages need to be more general to attract applicants to the organization; when the organization is well known and has a positive image, the messages may be quite detailed because applicants are already familiar with the organization (Collins, 2007). Other message decisions also need to be considered, such as media choice and timing.

Finally, research suggests that the manner in which the recruitment activities are carried out influences applicants. For example, applicants are less likely to trust recruiters from personnel departments, and are less likely to accept offers from them than they are from job incumbents or future supervisors, who are perceived as more credible and able to provide higher-quality information (Breaugh & Starke, 2000; Jablin, 2001). Providing more realistic or complete information influences not only acceptance of offers, but also outcomes like job satisfaction and turnover (Ryan & Tippins, 2004). These and a variety of other characteristics of the recruitment activities influence the recruitment outcomes.

Recruitment sources

The interaction of the recruitment efforts of organizations and the reconnaissance efforts of potential members occurs through the various recruitment sources that facilitate the mutual selection process. The level of control that organizational agents and applicants have varies with the recruitment source.

Organizations release a large amount of *public information.* Some information is of a general nature, such as annual reports, PR efforts, or advertising designed to project a particular image or "brand." Other messages are more specific to recruiting, such as application packets given to potential applicants. Organizations of almost every size maintain websites that provide general organizational information. In addition, they frequently include "careers" or "job opportunities" links that provide specific information about positions available across geographical locations. Applicants can access this information and in some instances complete the application process electronically.

Some public information is beyond organizational control. News coverage, blogs, and an increasing number of new forms of communication provide information directly to potential members without organizations being able to filter or control the messages. Organizations often attempt to counter negative coverage through public relations or issues management efforts. For example, they may post responses to criticisms on their webpage or create press releases to focus media attention on their positive aspects. In other cases, they capitalize on positive coverage by distributing the information more widely. For example, organizations often include on their webpage the fact that *Fortune* magazine rated them as a top employer, or *Business Week* said they were a good place for college graduates to start careers. Potential members can access both positive and negative messages as they make decisions about applying to the organization.

Organizations use a variety of face-to-face recruitment activities including *campus placement centers.* Many universities, especially large ones, have placement centers for students or alumni. These centers, some for specific majors and others more general, often assist students in writing résumés and participating in mock interviews. They assist organizations in recruiting by posting job opportunities and allowing organizational representatives to conduct screening interviews on campus. Applicants gain access to organizations without traveling and interviewing experience. Much of the job interview research reported in this chapter was conducted at such centers.

Job fairs are another common face-to-face recruitment method. Although some are conducted on college campuses, others are community or geographically based. Job fairs may be industry- or occupation-specific – such as a medical job fair – or more general. Because organizations pay for the opportunity to recruit from a larger applicant pool, individuals may have to register, but generally at no cost. Both career centers and job fairs provide recruiters and applicants opportunities to meet and make initial assessments of their mutual compatibility and can lead to follow-up interviews.

Rather than conducting the recruitment process themselves, some organizations rely on *employment agencies* including *temporary agencies*. These agencies recruit potential employees and then place them in positions that ideally meet the needs of both the individuals and the organizations. For lower-level positions, these placements are often temporary and allow the organization and the individual to determine whether there is a good match. However, not all temporary employees are looking for permanent positions; some enjoy the freedom of temporary employment (Sias, Kramer, & Jenkins, 1997). Employment agencies that focus on higher-level employees, sometimes called "head hunters," typically seek more permanent employment for qualified candidates who are interviewed extensively by the agency and the organization before being hired. Applicants have some control in the process by choosing to register with the agencies and by accepting or rejecting interviews or placements they are offered.

Organizations recruit through written materials including *paper or electronic publications*. This includes general distribution sources such as newspaper ads, or electronic job sources, such as Monster.com or CareerBuilder.com, as well as more targeted sources such as professional association publications. Although sometimes organizations place ads in these outlets to meet legal requirements or procedural norms of their organizations when it is already known who will fill the position, these sources do provide both applicants and organizations with opportunities to participate in the mutual selection process. Organizations choose where to recruit and select applicants from data bases. In addition to responding to job listings, applicants can join associations and attend conferences where formal or informal interviews occur.

A primary source for recruitment and reconnaissance is *networking*. Organizations network for applicants by having current employees refer potential employees. Applicants network for job leads through personal and professional contacts. A seminal article by Granovetter (1973) identified the most important networking sources for job leads. He divided sources into close ties and weak ties. Close ties are individuals with whom a person has frequent communication, including parents, close friends, and co-workers. In contrast, weak ties are individuals with whom one has infrequent communication, such as a neighbor of a relative or a client or customer. Granovetter found that weak ties led to the most job opportunities. Weak ties were aware of unique opportunities including ones that were not publicly advertised, whereas close ties typically know of the same opportunities as the job seeker. An additional advantage of networking is that individuals can mention network contacts, which gives them more credibility as applicants.

Although organizations have limited control over recruiting through networking, the process benefits both organizations and individuals. The individual serving as the network link typically only refers potential employees who seem like a good match for the organization. In this way, the link filters out individuals from applying that they do not think fit and prevents organizations from spending resources on unlikely prospects. Although there are some contrary findings, research generally finds that employees gained through referrals or networking are more satisfied and have lower turnover rates (Ryan & Tippin, 2004).

There are additional sources where the recruitment and reconnaissance efforts intersect, but these are some of the most common ones (Yate, 2008). During this process, there is little opportunity for personalization as the organization is mostly attempting to socialize the potential newcomer to meet its needs, and the applicant, at least tacitly, accepts or adopts the organization's values and beliefs by applying. Certainly, individuals can reject those socialization attempts by going to different organizations. However, this does not change the organization; it simply creates a better match for the individual at a different one.

Personalization sometimes occurs during recruitment and reconnaissance if groups of individuals collectively go to other organizations because one is failing to meet their needs. For example, if an organization begins offering flex-time because it is necessary to stay competitive with other organizations in recruiting qualified applicants, then those individuals have collectively personalized the organization to meet their needs.

The recruitment–reconnaissance process does not always work equally for applicants. People from different ethnic, economic, or social groups may not have equal access to information about some of these sources and often do not have equal access to sources such as campus recruiters. Networking may be particularly problematic for many individuals. They may not have weak ties, and current employees may filter out diverse and unique individuals in their referrals. Limited access for whatever reason diminishes opportunities for applicants, but also prevents the organization from gaining from their unique perspectives.

In the scenario, Amari used the college recruitment office for a lead while Casey found out about the opportunity through networking. These sources were not available to all potential applicants, but are two common ways the mutual selection process begins as part of organizational anticipatory socialization.

Part 2: Selection process

Although presented as if they occur separately, recruitment and reconnaissance continue during the selection process. Organizational representatives continue to recruit applicants and the applicants continue to seek information until they have made employment decisions. The difference in focus is that the recruitment and reconnaissance process concerns decisions to apply to an organization while the selection process concerns decisions to make and/or accept offers to join. Two communication activities dominate the selection process: written materials including résumés and cover letters, and oral communication during interviews.

Résumés and cover letters

Résumés and cover letters are a very important part of the communication during the selection process. These documents serve somewhat conflicting goals. Applicants use them to make positive first impressions to secure job interviews. Organizational representatives use them to eliminate less-qualified applicants from further consideration. There is an over-abundance of information on the World Wide Web about preparing these documents: a Google search produced over 5 millions hits concerning résumés and cover letters.

Much of the information from scholars is descriptive of what to include or exclude in these documents (Hutchinson & Brefka, 1997). Because "best practices" change regularly, the descriptions are often very general. For example, most scholars and practitioners agree that résumés should include contact information, education, work experience, activities/awards, and references and encourage use of active voice in describing job duties. Some suggest putting "goal" or "career goal" statements into only one document, the cover letter more often than the résumé. However, due to the ease with which individuals can edit and print specialized résumés and cover letters, this may be more of a matter of preference.

Most websites on résumés and cover letters offer similar advice to the scholarly research. For example, two easily accessible websites, Jobweb.com (2009) and Jobstar.com (2009), recommend including the same types of information as the research mentioned above. They differ from the scholarly research in that they provide more directives, explicitly stating what applicants should and should not do. Websites like these also provide templates for résumés and cover letters and in some cases provide different templates for different occupations.

Problematic in the popular advice, and to a lesser degree the scholarly research, is the apparent assumption that there is a preferred or ideal format for résumés, implying that "correct" résumés guarantee applicants interviews. Scholars and practitioners would likely deny the validity of this assumption. There certainly are, however, ways that résumés and cover letters eliminate individuals from consideration, from simple things like a lack of proofreading to broader problems like failing to show a relationship between personal qualifications and the job. Regardless, résumés cannot guarantee job interviews since factors like the number of openings and the size of the applicant pool and other contextual factors have a greater impact.

Research suggests that résumés have an important impact on the selection process. For example, work or educational experiences that are closely related to the job description increase the likelihood of positive evaluations; in addition, using impression management techniques, such as describing concrete examples of accomplishments, examples of positive feedback from customers, and stating interests in career development, increase the evaluation of the person as confident and hirable (Knouse, 1994). Recent graduates with limited work experience are more likely to receive job interviews with a one-page instead of two-page résumé, specific instead of general objectives, and higher grade-point-averages, along with relevant course work and accomplishments (Thoms, McMasters, Roberts, & Dombkowski, 1999).

Because stereotypes often lead to discrimination against certain individuals, written communication does not create equality during the selection process. For example, married men and women were evaluated more positively than single men and women with the same résumé qualifications (Oliphant & Alexander, 1982). Although there is conflicting evidence over whether women generally receive higher or lower evaluations, the applicants' gender affects how résumés are evaluated. Applicants with the same qualifications received higher ratings for same-gender stereotyped work (woman applying for day-care director; man applying for mechanical engineering) and lower evaluations for opposite-gender stereotyped work (Muchinsky & Harris, 1977). This pattern of reinforcing occupational stereotypes occurred primarily in evaluating applicants of average ability; there was not a significant pattern related to gender of the high-quality applicants. Taken together, the research suggests that some individuals may be excluded from the hiring process based on information contained in written communication.

Although much of the research and advice is consistent, some research is contradictory or dated. This makes it difficult to know whether there have been any changes in attitudes, expectations, and behaviors over time. Overall, written communication is an important part of the selection process although exact effects seem difficult to determine.

Screening interviews

Much of the job interview research and advice is based on studies of screening interviews conducted under controlled conditions at interview centers, either in large companies or at university career centers. For the organization, these initial screening interviews serve multiple purposes, such as public relations and advertising, in addition to finding qualified applicants; at the same time, applicants gain information about organizations as potential employers (V. D. Miller & Buzzanell, 1996). Various scholars summarize the research on job interviews (e.g., Harris, 1989; Judge, Cable, & Higgins, 2000). Some of the more important findings follow.

Job interviews are frequently viewed as a process for determining person-to-job fit (P-J) (Adkins, Russell, & Werbel, 1994). Given the managerial bias of this research, the focus has been on the organizational agents determining whether applicants have the requisite knowledge, skills, and experience to fill the job. Additional research has focused on evaluating person-to-organization fit (P-O). Those favoring P-O fit argue that fitting into the organizational culture is more important than particular job skills, particularly in cases where much of the work is learned on the job (Jablin, 2001). Despite these goals, typical unstructured interviews carried out without conducting a job analysis are not effective in hiring applicants who perform well and remain in jobs (Judge et al., 2000).

A large body of research focuses on improving job interviews, at least from the organization's perspective. For example, a meta-analysis of studies found that interviews conducted using questions based on a formal job analysis provided more valid results than those conducted with an informal or armchair assessment (Wiesner & Cronshaw, 1988). Harris (1989) reports that structured interviews, in which the same questions are asked of all job candidates, provide a more valid selection process than unstructured interviews.

Studies of structured interviews compare types of interview questions. Situational interviews (SIs) ask applicants what they would do in hypothetical scenarios, such as: "What would you do if you found out there was a conflict between two groups of your subordinates about whether to have a team recognition dinner?" Past-behavior interviews (PBIs) ask applicants to illustrate how they have responded to certain situations or problems in their previous experience, such as: "Tell me about a time when you managed a conflict between members of your team or workgroup." In a typical study, Krajewski, Goffin, McCarthy, Rothstein, and Johnston (2006) found that the PBI was a better predictor of supervisors' ratings of work performance a year later than was the SI.

Jablin (2001) summarizes a number of studies that examine the impact of the communication behaviors of applicants. For example, individuals whose nonverbal behavior matches interview expectations are more likely to be rated positively. So, for example, applicants who show nonverbal immediacy by looking at interviewers when both speaking and listening and who acknowledge that they are attending and understanding by nodding their heads or responding with "uh-huh" at appropriate times are perceived more positively. Applicants who are allowed to talk uninterrupted are more satisfied with the process. Applicants who talk more (up to a point) are generally rated better.

Some research is a bit disheartening. Although applicants might expect to speak the majority of the time during the interviews, research consistently shows that interviewers dominate by talking 60–80 percent of the time. In addition, interviewers typically make their decisions about whether the applicants should continue to the next level during the first few minutes, but tend to talk the most during that time and ask closed-ended questions that provide the applicants little opportunity to speak and create an impression. Interviewers also tend to weigh negative information, especially if it is revealed early in the conversation, more heavily than positive information. This most likely relates to the fact that, in many instances, interviewers are looking for a reason to reject candidates due to an over-abundance of applicants.

Given the strong managerial bias in the job interview research, a few scholars, such as Ralston and Kirkwood (1995), have focused attention on making interviews more like conversation between equals. They argue that creating a communication exchange between equals creates situations in which both parties, the organizational representatives and applicants, gain the information they need to make informed decisions. There is evidence that interviews that appear to be more like a conversation between equals are more likely to lead to positive evaluations and additional interviews. In a complex interaction analysis, Engler-Parish and Millar (1989) found that conversations coded as between equals (response–response) rather than as between a supervisor and subordinate (question–response) were rated more positively. Unfortunately there is often a push by interviewers to get applicants to talk and a pull by applicants to get interviewers to talk so that both parties believe the other is resisting the desired interaction.

Amari experienced many common characteristics of screening interviews, such as being given little time to talk during the first part as the interviewer dominated the conversation. Later, it turned into more of a discussion between equals and Amari responded positively to this compared to other interviews. The scholarship on interviews examined so far focuses almost entirely on face-to-face initial screening interviews, ignoring phone interviews like Casey's. In addition, although for some entry-level positions this initial interview is the only one and results in a decision on whether to offer the candidate a job, for many positions there are second or on-site interviews, something both Amari and Casey experienced.

Follow-up/on-site interviews

Far less research examines second or on-site interviews, although much of the advice and scholarship on screening interviews is applicable to both kinds. For example, researching the organization, demonstrating good communication skills, dressing appropriately, and so forth are effective in both interview settings.

In addition to being the time when organizations make job-offer decisions, the second interview differs from screening interviews in at least four important ways (V. D. Miller & Buzzanell, 1996). Whereas screening interviews typically occur at career centers, job fairs, or controlled areas in personnel departments, second interviews typically occur on-site in multiple locations while the organization is conducting business. Screening interviews usually last 30 minutes while on-site interviews involve multiple sessions that last for anywhere from a few hours to more than one day, especially for higher-level positions. Screening interviews typically involve two individuals; second interviews involve multiple interviewers and, in some cases, multiple applicants. In addition, screening interviews have a rather predictable format and often standardized questions. Second interviews are much more fluid and less structured.

Given these characteristics, second interviews offer a better opportunity for more complete information exchange. Applicants hear multiple perspectives on the organization and can use the opportunity to clarify information from the first interview or from unofficial sources like newspapers or acquaintances; organizational members are able to gain more information about applicants over the longer time period (V. D. Miller & Buzzanell, 1996). In essence, because it is much more difficult for participants to use self-presentation and impression management behaviors during multiple interviews over time, more accurate and complete information is likely to be exchanged so that all parties have better information on which to make decisions.

In addition, it is more likely to be during second interviews that applicants begin to personalize organizations. It is not unusual for applicant preferences to be taken into account during these interviews. Sometimes negotiations of duties and salaries occur. By stating preferences, applicants influence the specific offer in some cases.

While making it to the second interview greatly increases the likelihood of an offer, the process is still full of potential opportunities and pitfalls. Simply maintaining a schedule at this time can be problematic when a series of individual and group interviews occur back to back. The experience can be tiring and draining. When meals are included there can be problems of ordering food that is messy to eat and the potential to drink alcohol. There are often infamous organizational stories about applicants who drank too much at a meal or social gathering and demonstrated a side of their personality that prevented them from receiving offers.

Another problem more likely to occur during all-day interviews is that conversations often move to topics about which it would be illegal for employers to ask questions. The laws enforced by the Equal Employment Opportunity Commission (EEOC) in the USA make it illegal to discriminate on basis of race, color, religion, sex, national origin, disability, or age, among other issues (US EEOC, 2004). As such, a wide range of questions are considered illegal if they could result in hiring discrimination. Many organizational representatives know not to ask these questions, but if candidates voluntarily mention a topic, the representatives can engage in a discussion of the issue. So representatives cannot initially ask about a spouse, but if an individual mentions a person, they can talk about the person. In fact, when recruiting high-level employees, it is not uncommon for organizations to provide programs like spousal or partner accommodations. However, whether the applicant brings up the subject (e.g., I'm pregnant) or an illegal question is asked during an all-day interview, it can be difficult to respond appropriately.

Overall, it is during second or on-site interviews that more information is exchanged and employment decisions are made. Organizational representatives and applicants come to decisions about whether to extend offers or accept them if offered. For both Amari and Casey, it was at lunch during an on-site interview that topics such as marital status were informally discussed. Amari seemed to adapt to the organization's socialization attempts during the process. Upon receiving additional information, Casey decided against joining the company, perhaps due to the inability to personalize the organization.

Realistic job previews

An unfortunate outcome of the process described so far is that both parties are so heavily involved in self-presentation and impression management that they may have limited accurate or realistic information on which to base their decisions. Applicants and organizational representatives mask negative information out of

61

self-interest. As a result, individuals may enter the workplace with very high expectations that will not be met. Organizations likewise may have unrealistic expectations of new employees. Many studies have examined the impact of unmet expectations. Results of a meta-analysis showed that unmet expectations frequently led to dissatisfaction and turnover in newcomers (Wanous, Poland, Premack, & Davis, 1992). The current recruitment process propagates this problem as organizations are concerned with attracting the best applicants, and applicants are eager for job offers.

As an alternative to this approach, some scholars suggest *realistic job previews (RJPs)*. In RJPs, interviews include not just the remarkable and wonderful aspects of a job, but also the negative and boring parts (e.g. paperwork). Since most jobs have mundane parts, RJPs are designed to help individuals make more informed choices since their expectations are more in line with reality. In turn, they are less likely to be dissatisfied and quit. A study of military personnel looked at two types of RJPs (Meglino, DeNisi, Youngblood, & Williams, 1988). The enhancement job preview attempted to enhance (improve) overly negative expectations, such as negative expectations for boot camp. The reduction preview attempted to reduce (lower) overly optimistic expectations, such as unrealistic expectations about selecting specific jobs or geographic locations. The combination enhancement and reduction preview resulted in the lowest turnover and highest perceptions of trust and honesty. The enhancement preview did the second best, followed by the reduction preview. Those recruits with no realistic preview did the worst.

Research like this suggests a general drop in turnover from RJPs, but most organizations continue to present only positive messages throughout the hiring process. Most likely, this is out of fear that they will lose top applicants to organizations which do not present RJPs. This fear is supported by evidence of a higher drop-out rate of applicants during RJPs (Premack & Wanous, 1985).

In the end, applicants often have to find realistic information on their own. Those with network contacts probably have an advantage here. The level of realistic job information that was provided is unclear in the scenario. Casey seems to drop out of the process because the information received provided realistic salary comparisons for the two jobs.

Socialization and personalization

During the selection process the interaction of socialization and personalization can be intense, although much depends on the applicants. Interviewers' messages attempt to influence applicants to meet organizational needs. Advice books and websites rather explicitly encourage adaptation when they suggest applicants should answer questions so that they show that they will fill the needs of the organization or particular job (Yate, 2008).

There are opportunities for personalization during the selection process. A variety of negotiations occur later in the selection process, particularly during on-site interviews. It is possible for highly desired recruits, especially for high-level positions, to ask for higher salaries, spousal or partner accommodations, specific geographic locations, or a host of other things. This encourages the organization to adjust to their needs. Even part-time employees often personalize their positions when they negotiate work schedules as a condition of accepting jobs. Of course, many of these "adjustments" do not actually change the organization in significant ways since what is negotiated is often within organizational norms. And yet applicants do have the sense that the organization has adjusted to their needs.

Pre-entry: from offer to first day

An understudied area of the socialization process, pre-entry is the time between when an offer to join is accepted and when the person actually joins the organization. This period is frequently quite brief, a matter of a few days or weeks, but it can last much longer. In some cases, college graduates accept positions months before they graduate, or individuals are allowed to delay their start in new job locations for months to allow children to finish the school year. Jablin (2001) suggests three communication activities that may be important during this time: messages exchanged with the newcomer; the newcomer's efforts to develop a reputation through impression management; and veteran employees' efforts to make sense of the newcomer.

Regardless of the length of the pre-entry time period, there is likely to be some communication between organizational representatives and newcomers. In my department, we accept graduate students into our program in late winter, but they arrive in late summer. Throughout those months they receive various mailings including mundane information such as how to get a parking sticker and more critical information like their teaching and advisor assignments. Some come for campus visits and we assist them in finding housing and acclimating to the community. Jablin (2001) suggests that the nature of this communication, such as whether it is supportive or not, sets a trajectory or tone for individuals' future organizational participation.

Although originally used in a different context, the term anticipatory impression management provides an appropriate label for a new hire's communication during pre-entry (Elsbach, Sutton, & Principe, 1998). During pre-entry, a thank-you note to individuals involved in the interview process, a common interview recommendation, begins creating an impression of the newcomer. Promptly responding to emails or requests for information creates a different impression from having to receive multiple reminders. Spending some time on site, but not too much time, creates an impression of a conscientious but not too eager employee. Through various interactions, newcomers create impressions on established organizational members.

While newcomers attempt to manage impressions, established employees must make sense of the newcomers. Newcomers are a source of uncertainty for veteran employees (Gallagher & Sias, 2009). They pay attention to the new members' impression management messages or, in the case where such messages are lacking, they make sense based on their absence. Because sense-making is driven only by plausibility (Weick, 1995), veteran employees may create inaccurate understandings of newcomers. As a result, even though newcomers did not actively participate in creating their reputations, they may have difficulty changing the ones the veterans created, which may work as self-fulfilling prophecies.

As mentioned, the pre-entry period is rarely studied. It would not be surprising to find that, in most cases, the pre-entry period has limited impact on either new members or veterans. Due to its brevity and the limited interaction involved in most instances, its influence probably pales in comparison to those of the selection process and newcomer entry experiences.

Different experiences

The literature reviewed so far suggests a rather equal playing field during the selection process, in which individuals have the same opportunities and experiences, regardless of their backgrounds. Instead, due to gender, marital or family status, race, and a host of other characteristics, individuals often have significantly different experiences. The more obvious differences might be discriminatory or patronizing interactions from interviewers, perhaps including illegal questions. Less obvious differences might include being asked different questions or being given less realistic information. The focus on P-J or P-O fit that permeates the selection process may lead to more qualified candidates being overlooked because they are perceived as not matching an organization's dominant demographic or culture. Fear of these problems may lead applicants to behave differently, such as attempting to hide information about spouses or children during the selection process.

Organizational anticipatory socialization for volunteer members

There is little direct scholarship on organizational anticipatory socialization for volunteers. Some of the previous scholarship seems more applicable than others. For example, the recruitment process is probably similar. Organizations recruit volunteers through the same methods, such as public communication, websites, and volunteer fairs. Individuals seek information about volunteer opportunities through similar means, including networking. One aspect of the process that is different is that, since such organizations cannot use monetary rewards or career opportunities as incentives, they rely instead on factors like organizational support and anticipated pride and respect for the work to recruit volunteers (Boezeman & Ellemers, 2008).

Unlike paid employees, most volunteers do not submit résumés or go through formal interviews before they join. Typically, they are accepted based on their willingness to serve, after very informal conversations that hardly qualify as interviews, although there are exceptions to this. For example, community choirs might have auditions to make sure volunteers meet a minimum talent level. A volunteer must try-out to be cast in a community theater production, although those wishing to help with set construction or ushering are probably accepted without much scrutiny. By contrast, individuals volunteering to work with children may be subject to interviews, along with background and reference checks.

Even though the selection process is typically less formal, it still is a mutual selection process. The organization may determine that potential volunteers are not suitable because their skills or availability do not meet organizational needs. During informal reconnaissance, potential volunteers may decide that an organization is not what they expected and not pursue volunteering. So while, for employment, organizations typically have more control over the selection process and routinely reject many wishing to join, volunteer organizations often face the opposite situation. The volunteers, who may decide not to join due to other obligations or due to an unfavorable evaluation of the organization, probably have more control over membership decisions because organizations are likely to need them.

Conclusions

The scholarship on the recruiting and selection processes of organizational anticipatory socialization is often descriptive and fails to consider the interaction of socialization and personalization. During this phase, socialization is probably the predominant activity, especially for entry-level roles. The organizations' recruitment efforts indicate the characteristics they want and need from potential members, as well as what they offer applicants in return. The individuals who want to join most often represent themselves as possessing those qualities in their résumés and during interviews, particularly when individuals are searching for their first "real jobs" out of college. As a result, individuals typically adapt to organizational norms and expectations far more than organizations adapt to the individuals.

Personalization does occur during organizational anticipatory socialization under a variety of circumstances. When there are many openings and few applicants, organizations are more likely to adapt to applicants. For example, many organizations with a large percentage of entry-level service jobs (retail, food service) adapt to potential employees' schedules, especially those of part-time employees, and pay them higher than minimum wages. In recruiting higher-level or skilled employees, organizations often adapt to recruits by offering extra salaries or benefits, negotiating job duties, or offering spousal or partner accommodations. Organizations may also adapt to the collective needs of the applicant pool. The additions of flex-time or on-site daycare are responses to needs of current and future employees.

If and when both the individual and the organizational representatives determine that there is a good person-to-organization or person-to-job fit, the mutual decision making process ends. Illustrative of the mutual process, Amari is prepared to accept a job offer while Casey plans to reject one. When individuals accept offers, they become new organizational members. Those newcomer experiences are the topic of the next chapter.

4

Organizational Encounter

Dakota's first week full-time at the bank was tiring. First, there were two days of training with other new employees at the bank's training center. The first morning included the bank's history and values. A vice president even spoke for a few minutes before lunch. After lunch the training turned to teller transactions and customer service. This was more valuable as the trainees practiced what they were taught at mock teller stations. The next morning's training was even more interesting. It dealt with security and safety procedures. While applying, Dakota never thought about people attempting to cash fraudulent checks and certainly not about what to do if a robber demanded money. It was probably good to be told repeatedly, "Give them the money. Don't risk your life." After lunch, there were tests, some on the computer and some conducting transactions and balancing the drawer. At the end of the day, each trainee was told which branch to report to the following morning and reminded of the proper "uniform" – a dress-code with narrow parameters.

Dakota was assigned to shadow an experienced teller, Madison, the whole next day. It was awkward looking over someone's shoulder. Some customers asked what was going on, but others simply said, "You must be in training." During the morning, Dakota was surprised when Madison explained some shortcuts they used to speed up processing regular customers; some of these were in direct opposition to the official training. In the afternoon, Dakota interacted with customers and even used some shortcuts with Madison's approval. By the day's end, Dakota realized how much time was spent standing in this job. The shoes that seemed so comfortable in the morning really hurt.

The following day Dakota was assigned the window next to Madison. Most transactions went quickly and easily. Occasionally, Dakota asked Madison about how to do something that was not covered in the training or just to make sure it was appropriate to use a shortcut. By the day's end, it was obvious that Dakota needed different shoes.

The next day was more of the same. Lunch with two other tellers was the day's highlight. Even though they did not talk about work much, Dakota picked up a few pointers about the teller supervisor and felt these co-workers could be friends.[1]

The process of entering an organization is called organizational encounter or entry. The most researched part of the socialization process, organizational encounter has been explored through a variety of frames or theories. This chapter explores four of those frames: socialization strategies, uncertainty management, sense-making process, and role negotiation. Although these approaches overlap, each offers unique insights as well. Rather than attempting to integrate them, the four perspectives are presented sequentially, while recognizing they occur simultaneously.

Socialization strategies

The approach with the longest history explores socialization strategies organizations use to bring in new members. The seminal piece, by Van Maanen and Schein (1979), presents a theory of socialization based on the premise that being newcomers is

---

1   The author thanks his son and DiSanza (1995) for many of the ideas included in this scenario.

stressful and that the strategies that organizations use to teach newcomers their organizational roles have important long-term effects on them. As such, this research focuses on the organization's socialization efforts and pays little attention to newcomers' personalization efforts.

Strategies

According to Van Maanen and Schein (1979), organizations, either consciously or unconsciously, choose from each of six different pairs of socialization strategies. These choices impact the organizational roles individuals assume. One choice is between *group* or *individual* socialization. In group socialization, a collection of newcomers are put through the same orientation or training simultaneously. Images that likely come to mind might be a room with dozens or hundreds of employees listening to presentations, or a drill sergeant or a sorority leader putting new recruits through training. In contrast, individual socialization involves putting each newcomer through his/her own individual orientation or training. Here the image is of a one-on-one encounter with one individual listening and asking questions while the trainer does the instruction.

As valuable as this distinction is, it creates a false-dichotomy. Although individual socialization might be used by itself, most group socialization is followed by individual socialization. Like in the scenario, there may be a large group orientation that explains the company values and mission, explains routine procedures that affect everyone, and walks newcomers through the steps of enrolling in the benefits programs. After that session, as the newcomers move to their particular departments and jobs, individual socialization follows.

The second pair of strategies is *formal* versus *informal*. For formal training, the newcomers are separated from co-workers and trained in a particular skill or procedure before moving to the actual workplace. Like in the scenario, new bank tellers frequently train at a training facility before moving to the branches they serve (DiSanza, 1995). They practice on their own or with each other before dealing with actual customers. Informal training is essentially on-the-job training in which newcomers begin performing their job tasks immediately. They may receive some quick explanation of duties from a supervisor or peer, but then they work, ask questions, and learn as they go.

Again, this is likely a false-dichotomy. Although parts of the process probably occur as formal training, such as learning about company benefits or general job skills, it is impossible for the socialization to be entirely formal. Once individuals finish formal training and start in the actual work setting, they begin informal training. In the scenario, the bank tellers informally learned that things were done differently at the local branch than they were taught in the formal training.

With these first two pairs, it might seem that group and formal socialization are likely grouped together, as well as individual and informal. No doubt this is frequently the case, but there is nothing that predetermines it must be that way. In a small organization, there might be one newcomer going through some formal training. Alternatively, a group of new volunteers might be thrown into the work without any formal training.

The third pair of strategies is *sequential* versus *random*. This has to do with the order in which new tasks are learned. In a sequential socialization strategy, newcomers learn tasks in a specified order. In some cases, they may not be allowed to move on to the next skill until they have mastered the previous one. So, for example, during training a new teller may have to demonstrate mastery of deposits and withdrawals before being trained on how to redeem savings bonds. Often sequential socialization is part of formal training, although it need not be. In random socialization, the newcomer learns the tasks or skills as they randomly appear in the work, and so it is often associated with informal, on-the-job training. If the first customer wants to redeem savings bonds, the new teller is taught that skill first. If the next five customers all do deposits, the newcomer is trained in deposits. If the next customer makes a savings account withdrawal, that skill is taught next. Although the sequential socialization offers some advantages by starting with simple skills and building on those in a logical order, the disadvantage is that the skills are learned when they may not be of high importance. With random socialization, the skills are learned when they are of high value to the newcomer.

In contrast to the order in which socialization occurs, the next pair, *fixed* versus *variable*, deals with the amount of time allowed or spent on learning each skill. In fixed socialization, newcomers know exactly how much time will be spent on the various activities. So the teller trainee knows that an hour is allotted for learning basic transactions. The next hour is dedicated to learning transactions involving certificates of deposits and savings bonds. In variable socialization, the amount of time for each skill is unknown. If the trainee learns the basic transactions in 15 minutes, then the training moves on to the next skill. If it takes two hours to master complex transactions, then that is just how much time it takes.

So far, sequential versus random and fixed versus variable strategies have been discussed in terms of initial training, but both can also be applied to organizational role development over time. In sequential socialization, if the individual has a target role of being a branch manager, there is a specified sequence to reaching it. For example, the individual must be a teller first, then a teller supervisor, a customer service representative, assistant branch manager, and finally a branch manager. In fixed socialization, there would also be time periods associated with each role. The individual might have to be a teller for six months before becoming a teller supervisor for six more months before becoming a customer service representative and so forth. Pay raises might also have fixed time periods associated with them. In random and variable socialization, there would be no particular order or time periods associated with these changes. One individual might become a branch manager in less than a year after serving in only two different roles, and it might take someone else five years.

The fifth pair of strategies concerns *serial* versus *disjunctive* socialization. In serial socialization, someone experienced in the role is assigned to work with the newcomer. The experienced individual serves as the newcomer's temporary (or more permanent) role model or mentor. The experienced individual provides initial training and then is available as needed. The newcomer knows to go to this person whenever questions arise. In disjunctive socialization, the newcomer has no one assigned to assist in learning the role. Although this could be due to lack of management concern, often it is because the person who previously served in the role has left the organization or because the position is newly created and so there is no one who knows exactly how to perform the job. If the previous security officer left the branch, or there was never an assistant security officer, it is difficult to provide someone to serve as the trainer.

The final pair of strategies is *divestiture* versus *investiture*. In divestiture socialization, the organization attempts to strip away the unique and individual characteristics of individuals and replace them with the standardized characteristics the organization desires in members. An extreme case of divestiture is military boot camp. However, when a bank insists on a particular dress code, such as no facial hair or earrings for men and only one pair for women, and expects standardized greetings for all customers, it is practicing divestiture as well. In investiture socialization, the organization appreciates the individual's uniqueness and attempts to reaffirm and build upon it. An advertising firm might appreciate a newcomer's unique talents and not attempt to rein in the individual's unique expressiveness, or a bank might let customer service representatives develop their own approach to greeting customers. In many regards, divestiture is synonymous with socialization and investiture with personalization. Whatever distinguishes these terms may matter to theorists but probably is of little consequence in the workplace.

Outcomes of socialization strategies

Scholars emphasize that the strategies organizations use impact the roles individuals assume in the organization. Schein (1968) identified three primary positive outcomes that occur. Individuals who adopt custodial, caretaker, or team member roles generally adopt the organization norms and preferred behaviors. Other individuals may adopt more innovative roles, including content innovators, who change procedures to fit their individual ideas or preferences, or role innovators, who actually change the parameters of their roles. Although the outcomes are slightly different from those originally hypothesized by Van Maanen and Schein, the findings of scholars like Jones (1986) and Ashforth and Saks (1996) have found that the more institutional socialization strategies (group, formal, sequential, fixed, and serial) are associated with custodial roles while individual strategies (individual, informal, random, variable, and disjunctive) are associated with more innovative roles. In addition, institutional strategies are associated with less role conflict, role ambiguity, turnover, and attempted or actual innovation. Individual strategies were associated with more stress and intention to turnover, but less personal change and more innovation. This suggests that the institutional strategies provide more security and predictability for newcomers than the individual strategies.

Summary and critique

The socialization strategies approach to organizational encounter provides conceptual definitions for describing strategies that organizations use with newcomers. Research building upon this approach provides evidence that certain strategies are associated with certain newcomer role behaviors.

While valuable, the research has three primary limitations. First, this research fails to look at the actual communication associated with the socialization strategies, which may have a greater impact than the strategies themselves. For example, if during individual training with a mentor, a newcomer is constantly told "there is one way to do things here and those who don't go along find themselves out of a job," the individualized socialization may be associated with custodial roles. If the message during formal, group training is that "We want you to come up with new ideas. We even provide you with a few hours each week to explore new ideas," the institutional strategies may be associated with innovative roles. Second, the approach fails to recognize that most individuals experience combinations of the strategies, not one or the other. Third, this approach portrays newcomers as passive participants in the process. The organizational strategies seem to affect newcomers with little regard to their efforts to personalize the organization.

In the scenario, Dakota had two phases of orientation and training. The formal, group training followed a sequence from easy to more difficult tasks within a fixed time so that all trainees were qualified to begin working at the same time. At the local branch, Dakota experienced serial socialization by being assigned to Madison, but the training became individual, informal, and random. There were some contradictions between the formal and informal training, but it was clear that both focused on divestiture rather than investiture. From wearing the same uniform to following procedures carefully – at least the procedures of the local branch – new employees were encouraged to assume custodial roles.

Uncertainty management

An alternative approach to studying socialization views the encounter phase as an uncertainty management process. While the socialization strategies approach focuses on the way the organizational personnel treat newcomers and incidentally reduce their uncertainty in the process, focusing on uncertainty management spotlights how individuals actively participate in the socialization process.

Types of uncertainty

From an uncertainty management perspective, the newcomer experience is full of uncertainty. Scholars have defined various typologies of information that newcomers must gain to manage uncertainty in their new positions, using various terms (see table 4.1). By placing them across from each other, it becomes apparent that many terms are either the same or synonyms; others

Table 4.1 Types of uncertainty for newcomers

Choa et al. 1994	Louis 1982	V. D. Miller & Jablin 1991	Morrison 1995	Myers & Oetzel 2003	Nelson & Quick 1991	Ostroff & Kozlowski 1992
Performance proficiency	Task/procedures Image/identity	Referent	Technical/task Referent	Job competency Role negotiation	Tasks Roles	Task Role
Organization goals/values	Workplace frame		Culture/normative	Organization acculturation	Make sense of experiences	Culture/norms
Organization history			Organization information			
Politics	Power/players		Political/power	Supervisor familiarity		
People/relationships	Task/social networks	Relational	Relationships	Involvement	Relationships	Group
Language	Local language	Appraisal	Appraisal	Recognition	Performance Isolation	

have nuances that make them somewhat distinct, and a few are unique.

These terms can be divided somewhat parsimoniously into four main categories. First, there are task-related uncertainties. These include knowing what tasks are expected, the norms for completing those tasks, and the evaluation criteria for the tasks. This may also include learning some group-restricted codes or ingroup language used by organizational members, the various communication shortcuts groups use to increase efficiency, such as acronyms. Second, there are relational uncertainties. These involve knowing who is in one's workgroup, how to develop relationships with them, and how to develop relationships beyond the workgroup through networking. Relationships include peers and supervisors, as well as staff members and others. Third, there are organizational uncertainties. These involve understanding the organization's history and culture and its general behavioral norms. Finally, political or power uncertainties need to be managed. More specific than organizational uncertainties, these involve understanding who is influential, who to talk to in order to get things done, and who to show proper deference to in order to gain advantages and create opportunities.

Internal sources for uncertainty management

Although, as originally conceptualized, the experience of uncertainty caused information seeking to reduce uncertainty, this is not always the case. Individuals may use internal or cognitive processes to manage uncertainty without seeking additional information (Kramer, 2004). For instance, individuals use scripts or schemas for similar situations or people to manage uncertainty. For example, if in a previous organization "being on time" meant arriving 10 minutes early, a newcomer might assume the same is true in a new organization. In addition, individuals may deny the uncertainty exists, tolerate it as acceptable, or imagine information-seeking interactions in which they predict what information they will receive if they seek any. For example, an individual may decide it does not matter if the appraisal guidelines are vague and imagine that a supervisor would give criteria like "quality work is rewarded" if asked. Individuals may manage uncertainty by using these cognitive processes without seeking additional information.

External sources for uncertainty management

In addition to internal sources, scholars have identified external information sources that are important for managing uncertainty (see table 4.2). The most frequently mentioned sources are peers/ co-workers and supervisors. However, there are a variety of other important sources including other organizational members such as staff, subordinates, and mentors, and possibly other newcomers. There are also a variety of impersonal or public information sources. These include organizationally controlled written materials, like handbooks or webpages, but also media coverage not controlled by the organization. Other information sources beyond the organization might include customers, who are sometimes more familiar with procedures than newcomers, and family members and friends, who are consulted since they may be able to relate similar experiences that help newcomers manage uncertainty.

Methods of information acquisition for uncertainty management

Individuals have a range of methods or strategies, from rather active to rather passive, for gathering information to manage their uncertainty (see table 4.3). V. D. Miller and Jablin (1991) provide the most extensive list of strategies. In an overt strategy an individual asks a direct question of the source of uncertainty, such as asking a supervisor how to do some task. In an indirect strategy, the individual makes non-interrogative questions or statements like "I keep wondering if I should . . .," which allow that other person to provide information. In third-party requests, the individual asks someone other than the source of uncertainty for information, such as asking a co-worker about a supervisor. In testing limits, an individual deliberately (or perhaps accidentally) breaks a perceived norm in order to assess the consequences and

Table 4.2 Sources for uncertainty management

Louis, Posner, & Powell 1983	V. D. Miller & Jablin 1991	Morrison 1993b	Nelson & Quick 1991	Ostroff & Kozlowski 1992	Teboul 1994
Peers	Peers	Co-workers	Peers	Peers	Co-workers
Supervisors	Supervisors	Supervisors	Supervisors	Supervisors	Supervisors
Senior co-workers	Other members	Subordinates	Secretary/staff	Mentors	Subordinates
		Newcomers			
	Written materials	Impersonal		Manuals	
	Clients/customers	Outside sources			Friends
	Task				Partner
				Trying	Family
				Watching	

Table 4.3   Methods of information-seeking to reduce uncertainty

Berger 1979	V. D. Miller & Jablin 1991	Morrison 1993a, 1995
interactive	overt questions	inquiry
active	indirect questions	
	third party	
	testing	
	disguising	
	observing	observation
passive	surveillance	passive, without
		seeking

gain understanding of the situation. For example, by arriving a few minutes late, an individual can find out the real norm for being on time. In disguising conversations an individual makes subtle requests or self-discloses in hopes of gaining information, such as discussing how something was done in a previous job hoping the other person will explain how it is done in the new place. Two strategies involve no direct interaction with information sources. In observing, an individual watches to gain specific information, but in surveillance, the individual simply scans for possible information that may be helpful.

Although this list is extensive and a few of the strategies may overlap, there are two alternative strategies not mentioned. In an approach that parallels third-party information-seeking, individuals may read, listen to, or view various media to gain information. For example, reading a press release about the CEO may help an individual manage uncertainty in preparation for meeting him or her, in addition to other third-party inquiries of supervisors or co-workers.

Another approach that has been found to be quite important in managing uncertainty is passive information-receiving. Other people often simply provide unsolicited information to individuals without any request. For example, a senior co-worker may see a newcomer and simply start offering information or advice. This unsolicited information has been shown to be quite important in the way transferees and newcomers adjust to new settings (Kramer, 1993a; Morrison, 1993a).

Outcomes of uncertainty management

The value of uncertainty management has been examined extensively. Research indicates that those who manage their uncertainty, particularly by reducing it through information acquisition, generally have more positive organizational experiences. They consistently are more satisfied, more knowledgeable, and more likely to stay in their organizations (Morrison, 1993a, 1993b; Nelson & Quick, 1991). Gaining information to manage uncertainty is particularly important when individuals break occupational stereotypes. Overt requests, third-party inquiries, and indirect inquiries were associated with reduced role ambiguity and increased role clarity for women entering blue-collar, male-dominated occupations (Holder, 1996).

Summary and critique

Overall, uncertainty management is a useful theoretical framework for exploring newcomer experiences. With so many new experiences during the first days and weeks in the organization, the encounter experience is fraught with uncertainty. Through cognitive processes and information acquisition, newcomers manage their uncertainty. Those who successfully manage their uncertainty appear to be more satisfied and less likely to leave organizations.

The current research on newcomers' uncertainty management generally fails to consider three important ideas. First, uncertainty management is an ongoing process throughout an individual's organizational career. It is not something that is accomplished during the encounter phase. Individuals continue to manage uncertainty throughout their careers. Related to this, it is important to recognize that uncertainty management is a mutual process in which both newcomers and existing organizational members experience uncertainty (Gallagher & Sias, 2009). For example, veteran members are uncertain how newcomers will change their work environment. Through information exchange, both newcomers and established members manage uncertainty. Third, most research has focused on newcomers taking entry-level or their first career jobs after completing their formal education. Many organizational newcomers are older and experienced. Since research indicates that older newcomers behave differently from younger ones (Finkelstein, Kulas, & Dages, 2003), much more research is needed to explore the experiences of these advanced newcomers.

In the scenario, Dakota experienced uncertainty during organizational entry. During the training sessions, Dakota simply used observation and received unsolicited information to address task-related and organizational uncertainty. At the branch, uncertainty actually increased as Madison provided information that contradicted the formal training. However, by asking questions, Dakota was able to manage task uncertainty. At lunch with co-workers, Dakota learned about the branch leadership and culture and managed relational uncertainty by getting to know co-workers. Of course, Madison and the other co-workers were simultaneously managing their uncertainty about Dakota.

Sense-making process

Sense-making is an alternative approach to studying organizational encounter, although it has some commonalities with uncertainty management: both have to do with newcomers understanding the environment by assigning meaning. In addition, both view newcomers as active participants rather than passive recipients of the organizational socialization strategies. Perhaps the most important difference is that sense-making generally involves experiencing something and retrospectively assigning meaning to it (Weick, 2001), whereas uncertainty management focuses on proactively seeking information.

Sense-making by leave-taking

According to Louis (1980), an important part of sense-making during encounter is understanding or making sense of the differences between previous roles and the new role, a process called leave-taking. For example, college students entering their first career job often have trouble letting go of common student role behaviors like staying out late on week-nights or procrastinating because deadlines are known well in advance. They may have trouble behaving professionally. Similarly, experienced workers may have trouble letting go of a very flexible work environment in a previous job for one that is quite rigid and inflexible, or vice versa. Stay-at-home parents returning to work may have to let go of behaviors that worked well with children but are unappreciated in the workplace. This leave-taking is a sense-making process because the individual experiences something that is different from the previous role and must determine its meaning.

Sense-making due to differences

Louis (1980) identified three specific types of differences that require sense-making for newcomers: *changes*, *contrasts*, and *surprises*. Changes are objectively known prior to the change, not only to the newcomer, but also to others. For example, everyone knows that the newcomer will have a new role, new title, new office, new location, and new salary. Because these changes are knowable in advance, there should be little need for sense-making for newcomers. They understand the changes prior to their occurrence.

Contrasts are much more subjective in nature and experienced only by the newcomers. Some contrasts are unknown in advance. Contrasts amount to unmet expectations that individuals may or may not be aware they had. For example, assigned to an office with no windows, an individual may retrospectively conclude that windows are important. If, in the previous work setting, the rewards were associated with the quantity of work and in the new place the quality of work seems more important, a newcomer will have to make sense of the differences and make some cognitive or behavioral adjustments.

The third type of difference, surprises, is also subjective. What sets surprises apart is the strong emotional reaction associated with them, whether they were known in advance or not. For example, an individual may expect that working in a cubicle will be different from working in an individual office, but experiencing the loss of privacy and ambient noise may cause an unanticipated, strong, negative response that makes the work space intolerable. Having taught for 15 years, I never realized that classrooms were important to me until I changed institutions. Only when I taught in a room with bolted-down chairs that made it impossible for students to work in groups or in another that created two tiers of students, those sitting around the table at the front of the room and those seated in desks to the side and back of the room, did I realize I valued good classrooms. Fortunately, I did not have to change jobs to overcome this surprise. I simply moved my classes to better rooms. Thus, surprises cause individuals to make sense of their strong emotional reactions to their new situations.

The examples of differences so far have been negative. Some changes, contrasts, and surprises are positive. For example, a new-comer may not be aware of how important supportive co-workers are until after the contrast is noticed in the new workplace. Moving to a smoke-free environment might be an unexpected positive surprise for a nonsmoker. The individual might be angry that he/she put up with smoke in a previous job and be pleased with the new environment.

Overall, newcomers experience difference in the new environments and then retrospectively make sense of the experiences. The process of making sense is critical to adjusting to the new organization.

Sense-making through communication

Because sense-making is a transactional process, not an independent process, it is through communication that individuals make sense of the organizational environment (Weick, 1995). Through communication individuals come to let go of their old roles and understand the differences between them and their new roles. Although sense-making occurs as part of the information exchange described under uncertainty management, two types of communication seem particularly important for sense-making.

Organizational narratives or stories are particularly valuable for helping newcomers make sense of their environment (Brown,

1985). Stories present the organization's values, identify heroes and villains, and socialize newcomers in a narrative form, instead of simply stating or listing information. Stories are often easily remembered because of the plot, characters, and action. For example, at 3M a story is sometimes told of an employee who made a mistake and went in to tell his divisional vice president, expecting to be in trouble; instead the vice president said, "Just a minute . . . I approved your project and if there was a mistake, we made it together" (Martin, Feldman, Hatch, & Sitkin, 1983, p. 444). This story suggests that the company values and supports its employees even if they make mistakes and identifies the vice president as a hero for reinforcing that value. To the degree stories like this are widely disseminated in an organization, they help newcomers and established members make sense of it.

Memorable messages are a second important type of sense-making communication. Memorable messages are ones that are particularly salient to newcomers. These messages assist newcomers in making sense of the organization by providing information about its norms, values, expectations, rules, and requirements; they emphasize the importance of the interpersonal context and social network linkages, especially to higher-status organizational agents, as a place to learn the organization's culture (Stohl, 1986). The memorable messages are typically conveyed by individuals with longer organizational tenure, including peers, staff, managers, and higher-status individuals in face-to-face informal settings; newcomers typically perceive the message's conveyor as attempting to assist them (Barge & Schlueter, 2004). In addition, the messages often emphasize somewhat contradictory goals of fitting into the existing organization while standing out by developing individual abilities. For example, during an informal lunch an experienced peer might tell a newcomer, "Be sure to keep the office manager happy because she can make your life easy or hard, but never settle for mediocrity if you want to get ahead." Such a message would encourage accepting the organizational way of doing things (socialization) while simultaneously encouraging individual development to succeed (personalization). Through further dialogue, the newcomer eventually makes sense of this memorable message.

Outcomes of sense-making

Perhaps the most important outcome of sense-making for newcomers is the development of cognitive scripts or schemas (e.g., Cantor, Mischel, & Schwartz, 1982). Cognitive scripts or schemas are cognitive shortcuts that allow an individual to work more efficiently or quickly because they no longer have to thoughtfully consider the appropriate action to take. Relying on scripts or schemas is sometimes described as going on automatic pilot or mindlessness. So, for example, a bank teller quickly develops scripts for handling routine customer interactions. A particularly effective teller might even develop scripts for making it appear that customers are receiving personal attention when they are not. Through sense-making, individuals create scripts for managing their roles. The successful development of scripts is probably indicative of successful adaptation to the new organizational environment.

Summary and critique

Sense-making provides a slightly different perspective from uncertainty management for exploring how individuals come to understand their situation during organizational entry. As individuals experience their new environment, and particularly as they experience differences compared to their previous environment, they assign meaning to the new events. The development of scripts based on stories and memorable messages indicates that newcomers have an understanding of their new organization.

An important issue with this perspective is that sense-making is not an individual process, but a collective process in which individuals intersubjectively create meaning for a situation (Weick, 1995). The established members and newcomers make sense of the new situation together. Unfortunately, newcomers may lack sufficient background or work relationships to participate in collective sense-making and attempt to make sense on their own. Since sense-making is driven by plausibility and not accuracy, newcomers potentially come to inaccurate understandings of the new settings; they may focus on making sense of the wrong things. For example, a newcomer in an electronics outlet may focus on keeping the store looking neat when the focus should be on selling product warranties. Another newcomer may come to the conclusion that a certain co-worker is the supervisor's favorite because that co-worker claims it is true repeatedly, when just the opposite is true. If the newcomer had broader organizational experiences and discussed the topics with other co-workers, he or she might have made sense differently and reached different conclusions. So newcomers can be inaccurate in their sense-making due to limited experience and insufficient interaction with people in the new environment.

Dakota had to make sense of various experiences during the first week of work. There were differences that were unanticipated, such as having to worry about fraud or being robbed and the unexpected physical effort related to standing for so many hours. Dakota experienced contrasts between the formal and informal training. In the end, after the memorable messages from Madison, it made sense to follow the norms of the local branch rather than the training center and to purchase new shoes to ease the physical strain.

Role negotiation

A fourth way of examining the encounter phase considers it a role negotiation process. This approach emphasizes the interactive nature of the encounter phase lacking in the other approaches. The negotiation process is not what the organization does to the individual, or the individual experience alone; rather, the negotiation process is the interaction of newcomers with established organizational members.

Process

Definitions of role negotiations vary, with some focusing only on the conscious interactions designed to change role expectations or requirements (Miller et al., 1996) and others suggesting that any activity which alters the expectations or requirements should be considered role negotiations, whether or not either party is aware of them (Putnam & Poole, 1987). Role negotiations include not only task considerations such as what to do, but also relational considerations like the nature of relationships, and understanding organizational roles, such as where in the structure or hierarchy the role is located. So an individual might negotiate to perform certain job activities in the same way under two supervisors, but develop a friendship relationship with one and simply feel like a nameless underling to the other.

Most scholars who describe the role negotiation process present variations on the seminal work of Katz and Kahn (1978). According to them, the negotiation process consists of four stages. First, there is the expected role. These are expectations that the individual and others have for the person in the role. Second, there is the communicated role. The role expectations may be communicated or sent in whole or part. Some of the expectations may be accidentally or deliberately omitted. Third, there is the understood role. The individual may understand the role differently from what was the intended in the message due to noise that interferes with the transfer of information during communication. Fourth, there is the enacted role or role behaviors. Here the person may choose to enact behaviors differently from the received role by limiting or enhancing it to fit individual needs. The enacted role serves as feedback and becomes part of the expected role, as the process continues.

For example, department members may expect a new administrative assistant to complete requests as quickly as possible, but communicate that he/she has some discretion in prioritizing work. The assistant takes this to mean that jobs not identified as urgent can be completed at any convenient time within the next day. Department members may resent that the assistant paces the work rather than rushing to complete it, and sometimes conducts personal business when work is waiting. They may change their expectations and accept the slower work, communicate their disapproval expecting the assistant to change, or begin marking certain jobs as urgent to adapt to the assistant's pattern. Each approach continues the role negotiation process.

Negotiation tactics or strategies

In addition to understanding this general negotiation process, scholars examine the tactics or strategies used to negotiate. Tactics generally refer to specific behaviors or appeals used to influence negotiations whereas strategies are more global approaches to negotiations. Despite the clarity of these definitions, the distinction is often unclear as one researcher's tactic is another researcher's strategy. One of the more extensive lists suggests nine primary negotiation tactics: (1) inspirational appeals focus on the target's values and aspirations; (2) consultation includes the target in creating the role; (3) rational persuasion presents logical reasons and factual evidence; (4) ingratiation attempts to create a positive attitude or feeling within the target; (5) personal appeal makes the request based on personal friendship or loyalty; (6) exchange offers favors or benefits in return for concessions; (7) pressure tactics implicitly or explicitly include threats or demands; (8) legitimating claims support from authorities or organizational rules; and (9) coalition enlists support from others (Falbe & Yukl, 1992). Some common strategies include delaying, information-seeking, and logrolling (combining) (Miller et al., 1996). Individuals negotiate their roles through a combination of these tactics and/or strategies.

Outcomes of role negotiation

The outcomes of role negotiations can be quite substantial. For example, role negotiations can result in changes in tasks and procedures to fit individual needs, abilities, and preferences; help in coping with job stress; increase innovation and flexibility; as well as help organizations to adapt to external environments (Meiner & Miller, 2004). When changes are openly and consciously negotiated, it seems likely that the individuals involved will accept and be satisfied with the role changes. Sometime role negotiations occur without conscious thought or direct interaction, such as when an individual tries something new on the spur of the moment that changes a role or procedure. Individuals who, through their actions rather than through communication, negotiate role changes may be lauded, reprimanded, or ignored when the role changes occur without conscious negotiations or supervisors' consent (Jablin, 1987).

Summary and critique

A role negotiation perspective on the assimilation process directly explores the interactive nature of the process instead of favoring one side (organization / established personnel) or the other (newcomers). It explores how individuals use tactics and strategies to influence role expectations and behaviors. Another important advantage of this approach is that it provides an opportunity to clearly see the interaction of socialization and personalization. During negotiations, established organizational members are most likely consciously attempting to change the newcomers to meet their needs and wants, while newcomers are actively trying to change the organization to meet their needs.

Unfortunately, individuals are not actually always aware of when they are negotiating their roles. Individuals may accidentally do something different in their roles and then continue that way without being aware that they negotiated changes. A supervisor may accept certain role behaviors from subordinates without consciously considering that doing so changes role requirements. Due to this, a role negotiation approach likely examines the most obvious and explicit role negotiations that occur while failing to recognize many of the less apparent or subconscious changes that are made.

In the scenario, Dakota had very little opportunity to negotiate a unique role. The expected role was communicated, received, and the tests made sure that those expectations were learned during the formal training. During the informal socialization, different expectations were communicated and received from Madison. Dakota generally accepted the task role as received and enacted it accordingly. Despite this, Dakota was able to begin to negotiate a relational role in the organization. Madison and the two tellers seemed like potential friends. As they spent time together, they began to negotiate the nature of that friendship.

Encounter outcomes

Regardless of the approach taken – socialization strategies, uncertainty management, sense-making, or role negotiation – the combination of experiences during the encounter phase have a cumulative or combined effect on newcomers. These go beyond those already identified.

Boundary passages

An important overall aspect of the encounter phase involves boundary passages. Although organizational boundaries are more psychological than physical, and permeable rather than rigid, considering them provides valuable insight into the encounter phase. Van Maanen and Schein (1979) identify three boundaries: functional, hierarchical, and inclusionary.

Functional boundaries are generally departmental and/or territorial boundaries. Even though they are part of the same organization, individuals typically have a sense of the department (or function) to which they belong. In a bank, the financial advisors provide different functions in a different location from tellers. Hierarchical boundaries concern issues like power and status and who reports to whom. Most individuals recognize who is their supervisor and their supervisor's supervisor, on up the chain of command. Even in fairly flat hierarchies, it is not unusual to have informal hierarchies where peers recognize some individuals as more influential or powerful than others. Inclusionary boundaries have to do with a sense of belonging to the organization's social system. A person can range from feeling on the social system's fringe to feeling central to it.

During the encounter phase, newcomers assume some position in relationship to these three boundaries. Prior to joining, they are nonmembers. During the encounter phase, newcomers move to a location within some functional and hierarchical level. They likely feel as if they are on the social system's periphery unless they already knew people in the organization. Through the experience of the socialization strategies, as they manage their uncertainty and make sense of their new setting while negotiating their roles, their location within these boundaries changes. They continue to move within and across various boundaries throughout their organizational experience.

In the scenario, a number of boundary passages are apparent. By successfully completing the formal training and being assigned to a particular branch, Dakota crossed the first inclusionary boundary from outsider to member and moved from one functional and hierarchical designation, corporate trainee, to a member of a particular branch. Being included in lunch with the two tellers meant Dakota passed an inclusionary boundary.

Adjustment

Newcomer outcomes or adjustment are not restricted to the four different approaches. Rather newcomer adjustment results from the combination of socialization strategies, uncertainty management, sense-making, and role negotiation, although the findings are not always consistent across studies. For example, Mignerey, Rubin, and Gorden (1995) examined the effects of the combination of socialization strategies and information-seeking on various outcomes, including role innovation, role clarity, commitment, satisfaction, and the ability to predict supervisors' behaviors and attitudes (attributional confidence). Ashford and Black (1996) explored the combination of information-seeking, role negotiation, and framing the situation as an opportunity rather than a threat (making sense). Because studies like these use a variety of measures and populations, the findings are not always consistent. Nonetheless, they do indicate a cumulative effect on newcomers' adjustment. In the scenario, it was the combination of the formal socialization program and the seeking and receiving of information that allowed Dakota to make sense of the organization in negotiating a role in the particular branch. Looking at only one of these approaches limits an understanding of the entry experience.

Individual experiences

In focusing on newcomers' general experiences, much of the research overlooks how individual experiences may be quite varied. Many individuals do not follow the universal trajectories suggested by the research; instead, many times, individuals are marked as different and excluded from opportunities and never fully assimilated (Bullis & Stout, 2000). Often as a result of being from a different socio-economic class, gender, race, or cultural background from the organization's majority, individuals' newcomer experiences may be quite different. They may not be welcomed or may be over-welcomed; they may inadvertently or purposefully be denied important information (Allen, 2000). The end result may be that they have difficulty crossing various organizational boundaries and feel like "outsiders within" (Bullis & Stout, 2000).

Volunteer organizations

These four approaches to examining the encounter phase likely translate to voluntary associations with little need for elaboration. Similar to employees, new volunteers must learn their tasks, develop communication channels for gaining information, create relationships, and understand the organization's culture (McComb, 1995). Since some volunteer organizations have extensive selection processes while others accept almost anyone interested in volunteering, a few observations about the encounter phase for volunteers seem worth making for each of the four approaches.

Because many volunteer organizations urgently need volunteers, those organizations likely do little in the way of consciously developing strategies to socialize their volunteers. As a default, they probably use individual, informal, random, variable, disjunctive socialization strategies. Often volunteers are immediately thrown into roles with little or no training. A volunteer might be immediately put to work sorting food at a food bank or put to work building a set for a local community theater minutes after they show up. Larger volunteer organizations, like the American Red Cross or many religious organizations, often have more elaborate formal, group training programs. Even for these agencies, the urgency of the situation can cause those training programs to be ignored. When I showed up to help sandbag for the Red Cross to prevent flooding, I was immediately put to work with no training or supervision. Volunteer organizations probably have to balance issues like the urgency of the situation and the skill level needed to volunteer with the amount of training they provide. Putting too many roadblocks in the way before volunteers can assume meaningful organizational roles likely reduces the number of volunteers, but may be necessary when the skill or commitment of the volunteers is more critical than the urgency of the situation.

Volunteers experience uncertainty like anyone in a new environment. Although they may want to seek information to manage their uncertainty, it may be difficult for them to find the information they desire. Other volunteers may be equally uninformed, and supervisory or long-term members may be difficult to locate, making it challenging for new volunteers to manage their uncertainty. Similarly, new volunteers may be on their own to make sense of their experiences if there are no established members to assist in that process. As a result, they may develop plausible but inaccurate understandings of the situation that influence their future actions. For example, due to the lack of supervision or feedback, volunteers may assume that the organization does not appreciate or need them and, as a result, they may leave and volunteer elsewhere. Anything that the organization's personnel (paid staff or regular volunteers) can do to provide information to reduce uncertainty or to help them make sense of their experiences has the potential to help retain volunteers.

Role negotiations are probably not extensive in many volunteer situations. More often than not, individuals volunteer for a specific task or function expecting to perform it; they volunteer because they match the organization's values and practices and assume custodial roles. Of course, this is not always the case in larger and more structured volunteer organizations, in which individuals may wish to negotiate changes and move into different roles based on their previous experience and skills. In addition, there may be more volunteers for particular roles than available positions in some circumstances and so individuals may have to negotiate who will function in certain roles. Perhaps the important point for volunteer organizations is to make clear which positions are available for any or all volunteers and which must be negotiated.

Finally, boundaries of volunteer organizations are even more likely to be ambiguous and permeable than those of other organizations. For example, Kramer (forthcoming) found that, due to the fluid membership, it was difficult to determine who were current members, temporarily on leave, or no longer members of a community choir. Functional and hierarchical boundaries are equally blurred, with volunteers serving multiple roles in various functions and most hierarchical distinctions informal rather than formal. However, the combination of socialization strategies, uncertainty management, sense-making and role negotiation work together during the encounter phase for volunteers.

Conclusions

This chapter highlighted processes that are particularly apparent during the encounter phase. An organization's socialization strategies, the individual's uncertainty management and sense-making, and the interactive role negotiation process are particularly intense during organizational entry. It is important to recognize that all of these work simultaneously, rather than independently as they were presented here. Newcomers are experiencing the socialization strategies while seeking information as they make sense of their experience while trying to negotiate their roles. The interaction of these various perspectives needs additional exploration. It is equally important to recognize that these four processes are ongoing. They do not stop when the newcomer moves from the encounter phase to metamorphosis. Rather, they continue throughout the organizational experience.

The ongoing nature of these processes makes it difficult to determine when newcomers transition from the encounter phase to metamorphosis. Newcomers become insiders when they are given more responsibilities, have access to privileged or inside information, are included in informal networks, are encouraged to represent the organization, and become sources of information for others (Louis, 1980). While a few scholars have suggested time frames for this transition, it is unlikely that any particular time frame adequately fits the multitude of newcomer experiences. Instead, the transition likely occurs when two psychological changes occur for the newcomer. First, the newcomer must transition from feeling on the outside of the organization's social system to feeling on the inside. Newcomers frequently mention being included in some social event or activity as an important step in feeling accepted. In addition, they often no longer feel like newcomers when they begin to provide advice to even newer members. Being seen as an established member by newer members changes their position within the organizational boundaries. Second, and perhaps more important, the transition from encounter to metamorphosis occurs when an individual makes a psychological adjustment from focusing on making the transition to managing their current situation (Schlossberg, 1981). When newcomers no longer feel like they are in transition and learning their new jobs, they likely have made the transition to established member. The next chapters focus on how organizational members experience the organization's culture, develop relationships, and experience transitions as part of their memberships.

5

Culture

Morgan had enjoyed working at fire station #15 for the past seven years. It was interesting to see what stayed the same and what changed. To be sure, the line of command was still quite clear. Sometimes during emergencies when controlled chaos was the best that could be achieved, it was less clear, but those moments were rare and even then everyone knew to follow orders when they were given. There was still a strong sense of how booters should act during their first year. They were expected to be busy all the time, wash the dishes, mop the bay, and show deference to experienced firefighters. If they took a short break, they did not sit to watch TV or suggest changing the station and quickly go back to work.

Morgan enjoyed the respect that came with experience but could still empathize with the anxiety booters felt during their probationary year and sensed that the station's three booters found the firefighter role a bit more challenging than expected. Morgan remembered what it was like. Not only did booters need to show respect and positive attitudes regardless of the work, but they also had to learn how to interact with community members. They needed to act like they were in control and appear compassionate without being too emotional. It took a while to learn to save the laughter from nuisance calls and the sadness from upsetting situations like the loss of life until they were back at the station where they would debrief in a somewhat less guarded fashion.

One significant change was that, while the more experienced firefighters were all men, there were a few women in the ranks now. This led to other changes. With 24-hour shifts, it meant that there were accommodations made for sleeping and restroom use, but those were minor. The group tried to avoid stereotypical roles. Women were not expected to do any more or less cooking or cleaning than men. On calls, there was no effort to differentiate roles, although individuals tended to drift toward certain jobs out of personal preferences. The fire department recently enacted a family-leave policy that allowed women and men to take time off for the birth or adoption of a new child, but so far no one at the station had used the policy even though two men had recently become fathers.

For Morgan the most notable changes related to technology. The city's new emergency response center could pinpoint cell-phone call locations. Prior to that, it was often frustrating trying to respond to emergencies when callers did not know their locations. The new system saved time and lives. In addition, everyone had cell phones now. Since firefighters cannot use department phones for personal calls, cell phones allowed everyone to conduct business and stay in touch with family members throughout their shifts. The only downside to this was the occasional cell-phone ring that disturbed someone's sleep.[2]

It is implicit in the previous chapter that newcomers must learn to understand their organization's culture. A general understanding of an organization's culture is often indicative of successful transition from newcomer to full member. Various definitions of culture exist, but most agree that culture includes an organization's assumptions, practices, and habits, which reflect the values and beliefs of its collective membership. Although some organizational scholars argue that culture is something that an organization performs or does rather than something it has (Pacanowsky & O'Donnell-Truijillo,

---

2   The author thanks his friend, a Chicago fireman, and Myers (2005) for many of the ideas included in this scenario.

1983), most researchers avoid such distinctions and simply examine manifestations of organizational culture (Hofstede 1997). Perhaps a way to synthesize these differing ideas is to view organizational culture as both the process and the outcome of communication. Such a perspective, consistent with structuration theory (e.g., Poole, Seibold, & McPhee, 1985), recognizes that the organization's culture must continually be created and recreated through communication. Individuals may duplicate, modify slightly, or significantly change the culture during this process. Thus, cultural manifestations that an organization has exist only because the organization continually creates and performs its culture through communication. Individuals participate in this ongoing process of creating organizational culture throughout the socialization process.

Manifestations of organizational culture

An organization's culture is manifested in various ways including artifacts, individuals, language or stories, norms, and rituals (Pacanowsky & O'Donnell-Truijillo, 1983). Each of these contributes to members' understanding of the organization's values.

The organizational culture's physical manifestations are typically referred to as *artifacts*. This includes objects which communicate organizational values such as the company logo, historic objects, buildings, and documents. For example, the metallic lettering with a slanted E in Dell's corporate symbol suggests a value of innovation and cutting-edge technology, while Bank of America's plain block letters and flag symbol suggest the importance of stability and patriotism. Artifacts such as a statue to a university's founder or the maintenance of an organization's original building indicate a value of tradition and historic roots. Written documents and publications often explicitly state the organization's espoused values.

Special organizational communication is another manifestation of its culture. In some cases, *metaphors* represent important values. For example, an analysis of Disney Corporation language found that two metaphors communicated its dominant culture: Disney as drama and Disney as family (R. C. Smith & Eisenberg, 1987). Supportive of the drama metaphor, employees were called cast members, wore costumes, and were onstage when they were in view of guests, regardless of whether they swept streets, sold concessions, ran rides, or portrayed Disney characters. Supportive of the family metaphor, guests were families who expected family entertainment, and employees worked together as family members. The family metaphor proved problematic when it became necessary to lay-off family members during a downturn and so management emphasized that the appropriate metaphor was Disney as family entertainment, not Disney employees as family.

Organizational stories or legends represent important values and beliefs. For example, at the University of Missouri a series of stories revolve around a set of columns left from the original campus building (Kramer & Berman, 2001). Depending on which parts of the story are told, different values are emphasized. Tradition is stressed when they are reported as simply being left from the original building. Innovation and association with important people are highlighted when it is mentioned that the building burned down when an electrical fire occurred in this first building west of the Mississippi to have an electrical generator built by Thomas Edison. Community connections are emphasized when details of how the community prevented the columns from being torn down as part of a successful effort to prevent the university from being moved are included. Thus, the stories told and the details emphasized or omitted reflect important organizational values.

Another cultural manifestation is the portrayal of individuals as heroes and villains, typically in the stories and legends. Organizational founders are often heroes in organizational lore. For example, stories of Steven Jobs at Apple or Bill Hewlett and Dave Packard at Hewlett Packard are quite similar. They describe how the founders/heroes began the companies in garages and built them to multinational corporations. In some stories, lower-level employees are heroes for providing unprecedented customer service, such as a story of a FedEx employee who rented a helicopter to assist the utility company in restoring electricity after a snowstorm shut down a regional office. Villains appear in

100

stories as individuals or collectively as organizations. For example, many corporate annual reports take credit for their successes while attributing problems to environmental factors including the economy and governmental regulatory agencies (Clapham & Schwenk, 1991).

The members' behavioral norms are important manifestations of organizations' culture. Norms may be explicit, such as rules or policies, or may be implicit, and may be understood consciously or subconsciously. Norms are sometimes defined as the "way we do things around here." Schein (1968) provided a useful typology of organizational norms that emphasized their role in the culture. *Pivotal norms* are expected behaviors that are so vital that failure to follow them likely results in expulsion from the organization. Obvious pivotal norms in most organizations include showing up for work or not sexually harassing others. Less obvious pivotal norms might include having certain attitudes toward customer service or deference to authority. Pivotal norms indicate fundamental organizational values. *Relevant norms* are not as important as pivotal norms. Failure to follow them probably limits success in the organization, but does not lead to expulsion. For example, failure to attend company picnics or holiday parties may reduce promotion opportunities. Relevant norms still indicate important organizational values. *Peripheral norms* are more like habits, most likely practiced without much thought, that are a comfortable part of the culture. For example, an administrative assistant may make a pot of coffee each morning or there may be a norm of saying hello the first time employees meet during the day. These norms are the easiest to question or change if they are truly peripheral. The coffee-making duty may start to rotate among department members when a newcomer accidentally makes a pot after arriving early and others follow suit.

Some norms become *rituals* that express organizational values. Many organizations have annual recognition ceremonies for years of service or retirement ceremonies that indicate that they value long-term dedication and service. In organizations without such formal ceremonies, co-workers often organize their own retirement ceremonies. Other ceremonies celebrate productivity (top sales person), excellent service (employee of the month), or various other organizational values.

The artifacts, heroes and villains, stories, norms, and rituals often work together rather than independently in communicating an organization's culture. For example Rodgers (1969) tells the story of Lucille Burger, a young, female employee who challenged the CEO of IBM, Tom Watson, to produce his appropriate security badge before entering a particular area of a plant during World War II. Although some of the entourage believed Burger should let Watson through, Watson complied with the request and sent for his badge. To the degree that this story was widely disseminated in IBM, it was a cultural artifact that included heroes and villains, and suggested organization norms and rituals.

The story has been analyzed by a number of scholars. Kramer (2004) examined the situation as evidence of organizational members managing their uncertainty about organizational norms for authority and security in the context of the war. Martin et al. (1983) analyzed the story as a cultural artifact that served to reinforce the cultural norm of rule compliance at IBM. Both Burger and Watson become heroes for following the organization's rules. Mumby (1987) argued that the story serves a political function by reinforcing deep structural norms and power differentials in the IBM culture. Watson's organizational power is emphasized since he had a choice whether or not to comply with Burger's request, and by following the norm he reinforced rules that benefit him in his position of power. Each of these analyses emphasized that the story represents different aspects of the organization's culture.

Three perspectives on organizational culture

So far the discussion of organizational culture suggests a singular, unified set of values are expressed and shared among organizational members. This original perspective of a unified culture may describe some organizations, especially small or geographically bound ones, or perhaps the espoused values of founders or upper management. As scholars continued to examine the concept, it became apparent that a unified culture did not appropriately represent the complexity of organizational culture. In her book, Martin (1992) explicated three different perspectives that provide a more comprehensive examination of organizational culture.

Martin's (1992) first perspective, the integrated or unified perspective is consistent with the description above. Using this perspective, one examines areas of consensus and consistency across the organization. The focus is on values and beliefs that are embraced by nearly all organizational members. The emphasis on areas of clarity and shared meaning creates the appearance of a harmonious, homogeneous culture. The integrated perspective looks for an umbrella culture that encompasses all organizational members.

Instead of focusing on organization-wide consensus, Martin's second perspective, the differentiated perspective, focuses on inconsistencies across the organization. The inconsistencies result in subgroups or subcultures within the umbrella culture. Each subculture likely has its own unified culture (or mini-culture) with clarity and consistency within it, but the various subcultures differ from each other as a result of different experiences and interpretations. As a result, there may be conflict between subcultures.

Martin's third perspective is called a fragmented perspective. From a fragmented perspective, culture is complex and filled with ambiguities. There is very little consistency or consensus; when it occurs, it is temporary with a return to ambiguity and inconsistency. There is no shared understanding of these parts of the culture.

In explicating three perspectives, it is important to recognize that one perspective is not more preferable, valuable, or accurate. Rather the combination of the three perspectives provides a thorough understanding of an organization's culture. Thus, organizations have areas of common, integrated understanding, subcultures that share understandings but disagree with other subcultures, and areas of ambiguity where meaning is difficult to assign.

A study of the formative years of Microsoft Corporation supports the value of viewing organizational culture from all three perspectives (Andrews, 2000; G. L. Peterson, 2000). From an integrated perspective, there were a number of shared values at Microsoft at the time. For example, the presence of multiple and up-to-date technological gadgets in each office emphasized a value of cutting-edge technology and creative thinking. The lack of clocks and unassigned parking spaces indicated valuing working long hours. From a differentiated perspective, there were apparent subcultures. Those who bought into the dominant integrated culture considered Microsoft a great place to work and saw themselves as future millionaires, while those who were less enamored by it saw it as a "velvet sweat shop" with "golden handcuffs." A fragmented perspective provided a frame for viewing the issue of speaking to the case-study authors. Current employees were warned to clear any statements they made with the corporate communication department. Former employees were sometimes concerned about negative consequences from having spoken to the authors and checked to make sure that quotes could not be attributed to them. It is difficult to determine what these experiences mean in a great place to work. Combining the three perspectives provides a more complex and complete understanding of Microsoft culture than any one perspective.

An important advantage of using this multiple perspective approach is that it also allows for a more nuanced understanding of how individuals may experience an organization's culture differently. Individuals from diverse backgrounds may be more aware of the differentiated or fragmented aspects of an organization's culture and may form subcultures with similar others to assist in their sense-making. Recognizing those differences provides a deeper understanding of an organization's culture.

In the scenario, a unified perspective provides a number of insights into the fire department. There are cultural norms that everyone follows, such as working hard during emergencies but relaxing during down times. There are specific expectations for booters, including staying busy and showing deference to senior firefighters, that indicate that seniority is a departmental value. The unit seems to value equity as it resists stereotyping women into certain roles. From a differentiated perspective, there appear to be possible subcultures. Station #15 may be different from other

104

stations in some ways. The booters seem to have formed a small subculture although they may integrate into the larger culture after their probationary period. The older firefighters who never used to work with women may have a different set of attitudes toward them from younger ones who always have. Women may develop their own subculture based on their unique experiences. From a fragmented perspective, the new family-leave policy may be ambiguous for everyone. Since no one has used it despite being eligible, it may be unclear whether this is an example of politically correct policy or a real opportunity for employees to balance work and family. Recognizing cultural elements from all three perspectives provides a deeper understanding of the fire department's culture.

Management practice as culture

An important indicator of an organization's culture is its management theory or philosophy. Each management theory has assumptions that indicate certain values. To the degree that the management theory pervades organizational attitudes and practices, it is part of its culture.

Since extensive discussions of management theories exist in multiple sources, this discussion simply emphasizes how four of the main theories influence the culture. For example, *classical management theory* is the oldest of the theories developed around the turn of the twentieth century about the time of the Industrial Revolution. Well-known explications of this approach include Taylor's (1911) scientific management, Fayol's (1949) industrial management, and Weber's (1947) bureaucracy. Although there are important variations across these approaches, they all represent very structured, fairly rigid, and autocratic approaches to management. They assume that employees are motivated primarily by financial gains and must be carefully monitored and directed to maintain standards and productivity.

Research designed to support classical management theories led to the development of the *human relations management theory* after World War II. One part of the famous Hawthorne studies (Roethlisberger, 1941) attempted to find the optimum lighting to increase productivity, but instead found that any change resulted in improvements. In addition, the studies found that workers developed social relations with co-workers that influenced productivity norms. In the end, the researchers concluded that pay and directives from management were insufficient to explain employee motivation and productivity; social relationships were important motivators. Listening to employees and social interaction between employees were important aspects of organizational management.

During the second half of the twentieth century, the *human resource management theory* gradually developed. In part based on psychological findings such as Maslow's hierarchy of needs, researchers and managers began recognizing that employees were motivated by factors other than money or social relationships (e.g., McGregor, 1960). As the workforce shifted from manufacturing jobs to information and service jobs, employees became more concerned about opportunities for advancement and the ability to find fulfilling work. Human resource management focused on providing employees opportunities for job enrichment and added responsibility to make work more fulfilling.

Teamwork as a management theory holds somewhat different assumptions about employees. Teamwork can be an organizing structure in which people work in groups, and/or a philosophical approach. Generally, management sets a broad goal or vision, but team members make decisions, possibly including hiring or firing decisions and setting schedules. Rewards are given at the group rather than individual level. Teamwork has been shown to have many positive outcomes in certain settings. For example, teamwork at the Harley Davidson Corporation was associated with increased group cohesion, productivity, and commitment (Chansler, Swamidass, & Cortlandt, 2003). Alternatively, teamwork can create an oppressive work atmosphere when group pressure becomes a form of concertive control (Barker, 1993). In an electronics company, the team developed rules that were more rigid and oppressive than those of management, including publicly posting tardiness and attendance records and requiring team members to work long hours to meet productivity goals.

Although many organizations include combinations of these management practices, the particular approach has important implications for the organization's culture. The practices, rituals, and norms of a classically managed organization are quite different from those of a teamwork organization. Members learn to work with the management culture. If the organization's culture changes over time or differs from one department or division to another, it can be challenging to make sense of that culture. In the scenario, a classical management approach permeates the fire department culture. There are clear lines of command where those in authority give orders and others follow. The importance of hierarchical boundaries is reinforced by behavior norms that distinguish booters from experienced firefighters.

Technology as cultural

The last few decades have seen remarkable changes in information and communication technologies. The technology has changed how work itself is done for many individuals as robotics replaced physical labor or computers made the typing pool obsolete. The nature of these changes is not the focus of this discussion. Instead the focus is on the way technology has changed organizations' cultures by changing the organizational practices, rituals, and norms.

Changes in practices

New technologies potentially change the organizational culture by changing practices. For example, information systems allow for both centralizing and decentralizing the organization. Lower-level employees gain access to information that was previously unavailable to them. At the same time, upper management can monitor employee activities more closely, resulting in higher levels of surveillance. In most organizations, there is a divide between those with access to the information systems and those without access.

Our image of all white-collar office workers sitting with laptops or computers on their desks with internet access is not representative of broad worker experiences. For assembly-line workers, maintenance workers, and others who do not have desk jobs, access is quite limited. Changes in technology change the organizational culture and potentially create or reinforce subcultures.

Changes in personal relationships

Technology changes organizational relationships. While this may seem like a recent development, scholars have explored this topic for more than two decades. Technology depersonalizes work relationships as individuals interact via email or new technologies instead of face-to-face. However, face-to-face communication and communication through advanced computer and information technologies (ACITs) were roughly equivalent as predictors of employees' assimilation, and ACITs were more important than traditional information sources like company handbooks (Waldeck, Seibold, & Flanagin, 2004). Since ACITs include email, voice mail, and teleconferencing, among other communication methods, this suggests that the frequent and/or inadvertent face-to-face encounters that may have typified office interactions in the past are being replaced with electronic interactions. So, even though technology makes information more accessible and communication more flexible, it also results in fewer mutually shared experiences as individuals interact less frequently face-to-face, resulting in less shared understanding (Hylmo, 2006).

Changes in structures

Technology allows for more varied work practices which change organizational structures. In some organizations, field workers no longer needed to report to the office as often because they submitted reports and responded to supervisor inquiries electronically; field and office workers have different experiences as a result (Rosenfeld, Richman, & May, 2004). Field workers emphasized productivity and following rules and procedures closely while office workers felt more pressure and time urgency, perhaps due to the supervisors' presence. Office workers desired and received more feedback than the field workers, who perhaps felt somewhat unnoticed.

In other organizations, technology changed the structure by allowing telecommuting from home. Although employees viewed this innovative work structure as cutting-edge and visionary, it resulted in different experiences and attitudes for telecommuters and in-house employees (Hylmo & Buzzanell, 2002). Some telecommuters perceived themselves as not-promotable because they did not spend enough face-time in the office, and in-house employees questioned telecommuters' productivity despite evidence that they actually worked longer hours. The changing structure changed work habits as well. Despite interacting less frequently, telecommuters often felt that they must be available 24 hours a day; they often felt that the boundary between work and nonwork was blurred. In both examples, technology changed the organizational structure and, as a result, subculture differences developed as various groups of employees understood the situation differently.

Increased surveillance

Often unmentioned in discussions of technological changes is the fact that new technologies have made increased surveillance of organizational members, customers, or clients possible. This is due not just to efforts to improve safety through the use of security systems, but also to the increased monitoring of activities. In many ways, technology is making Jeremy Bentham's theory of panopticon control as developed by Michel Foucault a possibility (Foucault, 1984). The theory states that individuals will follow or obey prevailing norms when they know that their behaviors are being monitored. Technology has dramatically increased the ability to monitor behaviors. Consistent with research on call centers (Bain & Taylor, 2000), a student of mine reported that when he worked at such a center, supervisors monitored the time he spent away from his desk, how quickly he answered calls, the number of calls taken, the length of each call, and even the number of keystrokes per call. In many organizations, technology allows for similar monitoring of phone calls, emails, and computer use on organizational equipment. Many of us have heard rumors of individuals or whole departments being fired for inappropriate computer use. Although technology has dramatically increased management's ability to monitor, it likely falls far short of the panopticon some fear, as the physical effort needed to achieve it would be insurmountable and managers must develop relationships with employees or face resistance (Bain & Taylor, 2000). Regardless of the surveillance level technology actually achieves, its presence communicates particular values, for example concerning trust, which affect organizational culture.

Summary

Overall, technological advances change organizational practices and structures, thus changing organizations' cultures. As technology continues to change, organizational members must learn the organization's ever-changing technological culture. In the scenario, technology seemed to have primarily positive effects without concerns about increased surveillance. Firefighters were able to do their jobs more effectively due to the response center's new technology, which more quickly located emergencies. Cell phones allowed firefighters to be more connected with family and friends during the down hours at the station without violating department policies.

Work–family as organizational culture

The organizational changes resulting from technology sometimes impact another area of organizational culture, work–family issues. The way work–family issues are managed by an organization's management and employees influences the organization's culture.

Work–family interface

Although it might be possible to conceive of work and family as completely separate domains, the reality is that for most people there is a constant tension, stress, and overlap between them. Three primary stressors between work and family have been identified (Greenhaus & Beutell, 1985). The most obvious one is *time-based stress*. The hours spent at work reduce the time available for family; similarly, time spent with family reduces the time for work. Factors influencing time-based stress include the time spent commuting to work, the regularity or flexibility of the work, the time of day (which shift), marital status, number and age of children, and other factors.

Although time-based stress sounds like "you can't be two places at once," being in one place does not guarantee that an individual is focused on that setting. *Strain-based stress* occurs when factors related to one domain interfere with attending to the other domain, even when physically present there. This occurs when thinking about a sick child or elderly parent interferes with an employee's work or when a work problem distracts an individual from focusing on family activities.

Behavior-based stress occurs when behaviors that are appropriate in one domain are less desirable in the other domain. For example, in some work settings being self-reliant, emotionally reserved, and authoritative may be valuable behaviors, but the same behaviors may be problematic at home. Similarly, being nurturing, emotionally expressive, and participatory may be positive attributes in family interactions, but may be perceived as inappropriate in certain work environments.

Causes of work–family pressures

While the previous section suggests a typology of work–family stresses, research by Drago (2007) and others suggests some of the underlying causes of these conflicts. A primary factor is the historic *motherhood norm* that suggests that mothers should be interested in and willing to do unpaid care. This puts pressure

111

on women who work as full-time employees to be full-time care-givers, adding to work–family stress. A second factor is the *ideal worker norm* which suggests that professionals should willingly work long hours and do whatever it takes to complete jobs without extra compensation to indicate their commitment to work. This increases both time- and strain-based stressors. A third factor is the *individualism norm* which suggests you should be able to take care of yourself and your family without government assistance. This reduces advocacy for programs like affordable, at-work daycare that could reduce working parents' stress. Finally, a *consumerism norm* in the United States suggests that you should strive for a larger house, more expensive cars, more exotic vacations, and more goods and services, regardless of your actual need for them. Gaining those items is often treated as more important than maintaining balance between work, family, and leisure. These societal pressures help to create the stressors identified.

Individual coping strategies

Researchers suggest that individuals use two primary coping strategies to manage work–family issues (Ashforth, Kreiner, & Fugate, 2000). Some individuals use a *segmentation strategy*. They develop relatively clear boundaries such as not working at home and not taking personal calls at work. They often have rituals for transitioning from one domain to the other, such as the drive to and from work, or changing clothing for each domain. When emergencies occur, such as a child getting sick, or receiving urgent calls from work, they experience fairly high levels of conflict because it blurs the boundaries they attempt to maintain. Other individuals use an *integrative strategy* in which there are no clear boundaries between work and family. If they work at home, they may interact with family members throughout the day. If they work away from home, they think nothing of managing family issues from the office or taking advantage of a flexible work schedule to run family errands. They experience less conflict when an emergency in one domain impacts the other because it is routine for them to mix the two together, but they experience more overall stress because they seem to be on call for both domains 24 hours a day, 7 days a week.

Organizational culture likely encourages one or the other of these coping strategies. Some organizations expect separation of work and family to the degree that discussing children during a business lunch is perceived as an organizational norm violation. Others expect integration and provide flexible schedules and technology for telecommuting. Individuals are probably more satisfied and comfortable with the organizational culture when their individual coping strategies match those encouraged by the organization.

Organizational practices

The combination of these work–family stressors influences the work experience and vice versa. Although a management bias in research might focus only on the ways that issues in the family domain detrimentally affect work, a more complete perspective recognized that the problems flow in both directions. Family conflicts or stressors impact the workplace and workplace conflicts and stressors impact the family (Frone, Russell, & Cooper, 1992). This bidirectional flow is evident across race and gender groups.

The way that the organization and its members accommodate or handle these issues is an indication of its culture. A wide range of organizational policies have been created to help to alleviate some work–family conflicts. Some of the more common policies include flexible schedules, telecommuting, maternity/paternity leaves, and on-site daycare. The degree to which organizations have these programs and the degree to which they are formally or informally codified are strong indicators of the organizations' culture.

Contradictions

A common problem with work–family policies is the difference between the espoused policies and the actual organizational norms. In an important study, Kirby and Krone (2002) found that organizations may have very supportive work–family policies, but employees rarely use them due to social pressure from peers. So, an organization may provide paternity leave for new fathers, but men rarely use it because they are concerned that peers will be unhappy because they have to pick up the extra work load and supervisors will consider them unfit for promotions because taking paternity leave shows a lack of job commitment. This suggests the importance of examining both written policies and actual organizational practices to understand work–family issues as part of organizational culture.

Summary

Martin (1992) describes a company which is known for very supportive family-friendly policies. One executive boasted about an example where a high-ranking woman, instrumental in the development of a new product, arranged to have a Caesarian birth to avoid the product launch date. The company insisted that she stay home but arranged for a closed-circuit television broadcast to allow her to participate while she was on maternity leave. The situation could be interpreted from an integrated perspective as an extraordinary example of supportive family policies, as the executive saw it; from a differentiated perspective as the privileges of high-ranking officials over those in lower ranks; or from a fragmented perspective as a contradictory, ambiguous message in which it is unclear whether the organization supports or intrudes on family time. This example emphasizes that an organization's work–family policies and practices are an important part of its culture. The manner in which the organization and its employees manage these issues influences the experience for newcomers and established employees alike.

Emotion management as culture

Although not frequently included in discussions of organizational culture, organizations have different norms concerning emotion displays and emotion management. The exuberance expected or required of Disney World employees is in sharp contrast to the emotional neutrality expected in many office settings. K. I. Miller, Considine, and Garner (2007) define five different types of emotions related to organizational membership. Emotional labor happens when individuals express inauthentic emotions for the organization's benefit. This includes flight attendants pretending to be cheery to keep customers happy, or bill collectors faking urgency in order to motivate clients to pay. Emotional work occurs when individuals must deal with emotional issues as part of the job. For example, social workers work with clients under duress or hospice workers interact with dying patients and their families. Emotion with work takes place when interactions with supervisors, peers, or clients cause emotional reactions. These emotional reactions are often associated with either movement toward goals (positive emotions) or hindrances from meeting goals (negative emotions) (Carver & Scheier, 1990). Emotion at work is emotion that happens at work but is related to other life events. For example, concern for a family member who is hospitalized likely interferes with focusing on work. Finally, emotion toward work is a more general affective state, such as satisfaction with work. The organizational norms about the display or suppression of these various emotions are part of an organization's culture.

Part of socialization into an organization's culture involves learning its emotion management expectations. This occurs as organizations select individuals who meet their emotion management expectations, provide training that teaches those expectations either implicitly or explicitly, and then provide rewards and punishments to reinforce those expectations (Van Maanen & Kunda, 1989). This process is more obvious in some occupations, for example when customer service employees are taught to be positive and polite or bill collectors are taught to express urgency, but it occurs in most occupations to some degree. For example, C. Scott and Myers (2005) found that new firefighters learned to manage their own emotions during down time at the station and on location during emergencies, as well as ways to manage the emotions of the public they served. So, for example, firefighters attempted to maintain stoic neutrality when interacting with the public even when small children were involved; then they debriefed back at the station and managed emotions by calling loved ones after such unfortunate events.

The emotion management expected in many occupations is described as professionalism (Kramer & Hess, 2002). Professionalism generally involves not displaying too much exuberance and masking the display of negative emotions. For example, showing too much excitement about receiving a raise or promotion, particularly in the presence of others who are disappointed, is likely to be considered inappropriate; a more even-tempered positive expression of satisfaction is suitable after receiving positive news. Openly expressing anger at a peer or customer is considered out of place; professionalism generally involves masking the negative emotion by discussing what was upsetting in a neutral tone without displaying the actual felt emotions.

The impact of emotion management can be varied. For example, emotional labor for the organization's benefit is generally considered negative, especially when individuals lose touch with their real or felt emotions as a result (Hochschild, 1983). Expressing emotions can have either positive or negative effects on relationships. Expressing negative emotions can be a turning point for either relationship deterioration or improvement (Kramer & Tan, 2006). For example, expressing anger could lead to individuals avoiding each other, making negative attributions about future interactions, and creating downward relational spirals. Alternatively, expressing anger could result in issues being addressed and relationships improving. Finally, emotion management can be a positive part of a job. For 911 call operators, maintaining neutral control during the adrenalin rush of dealing with emergencies is actually part of the job's appeal (Shuler & Sypher, 2000) and passionately telling stories about work incidents provides relief from its mundane aspects (Pacanowsky & O'Donnell-Truijillo, 1983).

The management of emotion displays is part of an organization's culture. Emotion management expectations express organizational values and the behaviors are part of its communication norms and rituals. In the scenario, Morgan learned to maintain a certain demeanor at the fire station along with appropriate emotion displays for interacting with the public. Managing emotions professionally was essential for developing positive relationships with peers and supervisors and for continued success.

National culture and organizational culture

Because organizations exist in a context, the organization's culture is influenced in part by the national culture. According to Hofstede (1997), national cultures can be described along four primary dimensions: (1) individualism versus collectivism describes the degree to which the culture focuses on individual rather than group needs and accomplishments; (2) masculinity versus femininity indicates whether or not the culture emphasizes stereotypical gender roles, and segmentation between work and nonwork; (3) power distance relates to whether the culture accepts and emphasizes status differences and resulting inequities or not; (4) uncertainty avoidance describes whether the culture encourages information sharing to manage uncertainty or tolerates ambiguity. Along these dimension, the United States is more individualistic, masculine, with moderate power distances, and fairly high uncertainty avoidance. Japanese culture is more collectivistic, Denmark is more feminine, Finland has more limited power distance, and Israel is higher in uncertainty avoidance.

Although oversimplifying national cultures which are more diverse than this typology recognizes, particularly if significant migratory populations form subcultures, this does provide a basis for examining how the external culture influences the internal organizational culture. In organizations located in a highly masculine, highly individualistic, low-power-distance national culture, we would expect an internal organizational culture that favors those same values. The culture may be evident in gendered occupations, independent offices, and informal supervisor–subordinate communication. In this way the organizational culture reflects the national culture.

Cultural diversity as organizational culture

The changing demographics in the United States and other countries have changed the composition of organizations. Where in the past organizations might have rather homogeneous workforces that shared a national culture, more heterogeneous workforces exist now, particularly when considering gender, race, ethnicity, nationality, socio-economic class, sexual orientation, physical disabilities, and other population characteristics and the increase in multinational corporations. Individuals from different cultural backgrounds often differ in values, work habits, verbal and non-verbal communication, use of time, and a host of other attitudes and behaviors. Due to these differences, research suggests that culturally diverse groups may be less effective initially because they must work through primary tensions, but that, over time, diversity results in equal or superior performance due to more varied experiences and ideas (Watson, Kumar, & Michaelsen, 1993). Rather than discussing all the ways the cultural diversity of the changing workforce assists and challenges groups and organizations, the focus here is simply on how an organization's diversity affects the socialization process. Larkey (1996) provides a useful typology for considering how an organization's level of diversity influences the socialization process by identifying three types of organizational cultures: monolithic, plural, and multicultural.

Monolithic organizational cultures are dominated by one particular demographic group. This may be the result of occupational stereotypes, geographical location, historical trends, or other factors. On a recent trip to Alaska, it was not surprising to see so few African-Americans or Hispanics working as temporary, summer employees in the tourist industry. Although native Alaskans were always present, whether it was as tour guides, bus drivers, hotel and restaurant employees, or gift-shop employees, the vast majority of employees tended to be young, white, middle-class, and West-coast college-educated. The geographic distance and state's history made the presence of cultural diversity unusual even among tourists. Participation in a monolithic organizational culture is quite difficult for someone of another background since they may feel they are categorized or stereotyped as a token representative (Larkey, 1996). Even if the Alaskan tourist industry recruits heavily to gain diversity, it is unlikely to achieve much success because of the reluctance to join for those not fitting the typical industry demographic.

A plural organizational culture has more diversity in it. That diversity tends to be segmented into certain occupations or departments within the organization rather than evenly distributed throughout. The diversity of the entire organization may look impressive in terms of percentages of culturally diverse employees, but this is frequently due to their over-representation in entry-level positions, while the organization's middle and upper levels continue to be rather homogeneous. Entry into a plural culture is easier at the lower organizational levels than in a monolithic culture, but for those entering or being promoted to higher levels, the challenges of finding role models and mentors with a similar background make the process difficult.

A multicultural organizational culture is one in which diversity is common throughout the organization. Members of previously under-represented groups are dispersed throughout the organization's departments and ranks. Because of this, individuals are no longer likely to be viewed as representatives of a group and so their specialized abilities are more likely to be attended to than their demographic (Larkey, 1996). In such organizations, the socialization process is more likely to be similar across demographics since role models and mentors are available at various levels in various departments.

As part of the organization's culture, its diversity influences the socialization process. The culture can welcome and encourage acceptance of diverse perspectives and backgrounds or act in an exclusionary manner. Individuals from under-represented groups may lack mentors and role models from their same background or may experience extra scrutiny as trailblazers. In the scenario, the fire station appears to be beginning to make a gradual shift from a monolithic culture to a plural one. The presence of only a few women in the ranks suggests that it will be some time before department employees mirror the population demographics.

Nonetheless, their presence may make it less challenging for members of other under-represented groups to join.

Occupational culture as organizational culture

Another part of an organization's culture comes from the various occupational cultures that influence it. During role anticipatory socialization, individuals learn some occupational norms. They continue to learn their occupational culture throughout their careers from peers within the organization, as well as from peers in other organizations. Although it might be easy to think of occupational culture as only applicable to professionals who meet at business meetings or professional associations, occupational cultures are quite common. Lucas and Buzzanell (2004) studied the occupational culture of miners. The miner's culture was encapsulated in the term *sisu* a Finnish word that roughly translates as inner determination, perseverance, courage, and guts. The miners used this term to differentiate between heroes who epitomized *sisu*, villains who violated its values for personal gain, and fools who simply lacked its qualities. With miners frequently being laid-off and switching companies, this occupational culture of *sisu* was a stronger influence on their behaviors than the culture of the specific organization for which they worked. Similarly, occupational cultures for teachers, police, lawyers, nurses, accountants, and a host of others impact the culture of the organizations for which they work. Occupational cultures contribute to resistance to organizational changes when those changes conflict with occupational norms.

Culture in nonprofit organizations

Culture in nonprofit organizations is quite similar to that in other organizations, although there are important differences. Nonprofits have the same manifestations of culture as other organizations. For example, the American Red Cross (ARC) has artifacts such as its symbol and stories of its founder Clara Barton, its most famous and important hero, to epitomize its commitment to saving lives. The rituals and procedures of blood drives demonstrate it values safety for donors and recipients. Similar to other organizations, the management philosophy, technology, emotion management, national culture, and cultural diversity are also part of the organizational culture of volunteer organizations.

From an integrated perspective, the ARC has some overall values, such as respect for, and commitment to saving and protecting, human lives. At the same time, the ARC's various units have different focuses and, as a result, represent subcultures within the umbrella culture. The urgency of disaster relief promotes a different set of values and behaviors from the calm of a blood drive or a class in water safety. Finally, from a fragmented view, there are frequently uncertainties and ambiguities about financial irregularities in its past or its relationship to government agencies such as the Federal Emergency Management Agency.

Instead of work–family issues, an important factor influencing the culture of nonprofit or volunteer organizations is simply their status in the broader culture and in their members' lives. Researchers have sometimes referred to volunteer organizations as third-place (behind work and family) (Ashforth et al., 2000), life enrichment (Kramer, 2002), or leisure activities. The nomenclature suggests that these are less important than other life activities. Even though this is not always the case – for example membership in a religious organization may be the most important affiliation for some individuals – in many cases, membership in volunteer organizations is a lower priority than other activities. As a result, volunteers frequently drop out, permanently or temporarily. The membership fluidity creates a different culture for volunteer organizations.

The scenario makes no mention of Morgan belonging to any volunteer organizations, but it illustrates a problem. Often volunteer organizations assume 9–5 work hours for volunteers, and schedule activities accordingly. For people working different shifts, such as evenings or nights, or irregular shifts like firefighters or nurses, such schedules might not allow potential volunteers to participate. Given priorities of work and family, this likely limits the diversity of the membership of volunteer organizations.

Conclusions

Organizations each have their own culture. The values of the organization manifest themselves in its management philosophy, technology, emotion management expectations, work–family policies, and diversity. They are expressed in the members' behaviors, rituals, and communication activities. A thorough understanding of an organization includes recognizing a unified culture, as well as differentiated and fragmented portions of it. Portions of this chapter may seem to suggest that organizational culture is fixed and unchanging. Although an organization's culture is presumed to be fairly stable, it does change. A few causes of these changes are discussed in chapter 7.

6

Relationships

It seemed like less than four years since Jordan started at the hospital. Staying was easy because it was mostly a positive experience. Working in customer accounts did not seem all that different in a hospital from elsewhere, but it was challenging with all the stakeholders – patients, doctors, administrators, and insurance companies. Entry into the organization went smoothly. Jordan felt included immediately. The department supervisor, Shanne, included Jordan in some important decisions the first month. Although there were limited departmental advancement opportunities, Shanne offered suggestions for getting high evaluations and merit raises. They talked about their shared interest in jogging frequently, but otherwise did not delve into each others' personal lives.

Peer relationships were one of the job's most positive aspects. Being a small department, everyone knew everyone pretty well. Shanne called them a team and they worked together rather harmoniously. The very first week some co-workers invited Jordan to lunch and they developed close relationships quickly, discussing not just work issues, like how to convince an insurance company that the paperwork was done correctly, but also personal issues, like a co-worker's mother being hospitalized or the trials of raising teenagers.

Another positive aspect of the job was the relationship

between Jordan's co-worker, Kasey, and Shanne. Everyone recognized Kasey as one of the most productive workers, who also had an inside track with Shanne. Jordan and the rest of the group liked to take advantage of this. They frequently asked Kasey what Shanne might think about some idea or asked Kasey to ask Shanne about some difficult issue rather than bringing it up themselves. This gave Kasey informal power, but no one minded.

The job had only a couple of negative aspects. Sometimes work backed up and everyone was expected to put in some paid overtime. That wasn't the problem. The problem was that people expected everyone to work overtime on the same days. Working overtime on the same days made it easier to get work done. Usually this worked fine and initially Jordan made adjustments to be available. But the last couple of times the "overtime day" conflicted with plans that could not easily be canceled. The group seemed to give Jordan the cold shoulder for a few days after missing those days. So, even though Shanne said missing overtime was not a problem, Jordan usually made sure to be available even if it was inconvenient.

The job's most negative aspect was Jesse. To complete the work, Jordan developed contacts in a lot of different departments. Most of these work-related contacts improved efficiency, although Jordan also found a couple of joggers who were members of the local runners' club this way and joined it as a result. In contrast to these positive relationships, everyone dreaded working on claims with Jesse, the accounts-payable person for an anesthesiologists' team that worked in the hospital. Most of the time billing went smoothly. When it did not, team members tried every conceivable alternative to resolve the problem and only contacted Jesse as a last resort because, when they did, Jesse often become angry and belligerent on the phone. On more than one occasion after cussing out a departmental member, Jesse called Shanne to insist that the incompetent person be fired. Fortunately, Shanne and the rest of the group always supported the target of Jesse's wrath which made it easier to take. If it weren't for those two things, Jordan's job would be just about ideal.

The previous chapter examined broad issues of organizational culture as part of the socialization process. This chapter focuses on the personal or relational part of the process. It explores the communication relationships that individuals develop as part of their organizational experiences. It is through these relationships that they learn the organizational culture and develop a sense of belonging to the organization.

Relationship development in organizational settings

A variety of models and theories of relationship development exist in the interpersonal communication literature. A typical theory, such as social penetration theory (Altman & Taylor, 1973), suggests that individuals increase the depth and breadth of information they share with each other as they develop deeper relationships. Typical relationship models (Knapp & Vangelisti, 2008) suggest that individuals gradually increase their relationships through a series of steps or phases as they move to closer relationships and then decrease their relationships through an opposite set of steps as they become more distant. Of course, these models' proponents recognized that not all relationships develop in such a linear manner.

Because these approaches do not include an organizational context, they provide foundational constructs for exploring organizational relationships, but the organizational context creates additional issues and concerns. As just one example of a contextual issue, it is not uncommon for newcomers to feel that their new co-workers are a bit standoffish, as if waiting for them to prove themselves. Co-workers sometimes take this "wait-and-see" attitude toward organizational newcomers (Miller & Jablin, 1991), as well as transfers from other organizational locations (Kramer,

1993a). A nuanced examination of this phenomenon might discover it is related to specific contextual factors. In organizations with high turnover among newcomers, it makes sense for established employees to see if newcomers will be around long enough before trying to develop relationships with them; of course, this wait-and-see attitude may also contribute to the high turnover rate as newcomers feel unwelcomed. Alternatively, if newcomers are replacing co-workers whose work was sub-par and incomplete, the co-workers may eagerly accept any replacement. In this way, the relationship development is affected by the organizational context.

Because there are a large number of potential contextual factors that influence relationship development in organizations, this chapter focuses on one contextual factor, the type of work relationship. It explores supervisor–subordinate relationships, peer relationships, mentor relationships, in addition to more general network relationships. In addition, since not all workplace relationships are positive, it examines problems associated with negative workplace relationships.

Supervisor–subordinate relationships

Foundational research on supervisor–subordinate relationships conducted from the 1950s to the 1970s was summarized by Jablin (1979). This research focused on the characteristics of effective versus ineffective supervisors. Among other findings, Jablin reported that supervisors spent a third to two-thirds of their time communicating with subordinates; however, supervisors perceived they communicated more than their subordinates perceived. Subordinates in more open communication relationships with their supervisors, characterized as both parties being willing and receptive listeners, were more satisfied than those in closed relationships. Subordinates were more likely to distort their upward communication when there was a lack of trust and openness with their supervisors. Subordinates were more likely to interact with and trust supervisors with substantial but not excessive amounts of upward influence with their own bosses. Supervisors and subordinates frequently experienced semantic information distance (differences in perceived meanings) that hindered their ability to work together effectively. More effective supervisors were communication-minded, willing and empathic listeners, asked or persuaded rather than demanded or told, and were more willing to pass along information to subordinates. Subordinates who received more positive and complete feedback from their supervisors tended to be more satisfied in their jobs, but the quality of their performances influenced the nature of the feedback they received. Subordinates in higher-ranking positions or in fairly flat organizational structures experienced more open communication and involvement in decision making. Taken together, this strongly supports the notion that the experience of the supervisor–subordinate relationship influences the adjustment and satisfaction of new and established employees.

The previous discussion of supervisor–subordinate relationships is based on the premise that supervisors have an average leadership style (ALS) that they use with all of their subordinates. Although supervisors may want to believe that they treat all their subordinates equally and therefore fairly, evidence indicates that they do not. A line of research by Graen and his associates indicates that supervisors develop different relationships with various subordinates (Graen, 2003; Graen & Uhl-Bien, 1995). Originally called vertical dyad linkage, but later renamed, the premise of leader member exchange (LMX) is that supervisors develop one of three types of relationships with subordinates.

High LMX relationships, sometimes called partnerships or ingroup relationships, are characterized by mutual trust and respect, communication that is open and consultative rather than directing, concern for career and nonwork activities, and a sense of commitment, bonding, and mutual support. Many of these characteristics are similar to the descriptions of effective supervisors in the earlier research. At the opposite end of the spectrum, low LMX relationships, sometimes called overseer or outgroup relationships, typically involve low levels of trust, communication that is directive and focuses on work or task activities, and a sense of distance and lack of support. These characteristics are indicative of ineffective supervisors in the previous research. Middle-group LMX relationships fall in-between these two extremes.

Studies with a micro-analytic focus on actual interactions have found more specific communication differences across LMX relationships (Fairhurst & Chandler, 1989). For example, in low LMX relationships, conversations were typically brief, with supervisors more likely to interrupt and make suggestions to subordinates who then complied. This limited subordinates' ability to influence the outcomes or improve the relationship. In high LMX relationships, both parties were willing to interrupt each other and subordinates actively tried to influence supervisors, who offered support for whatever decision subordinates made. In middle-group relationships, power and social distance were more ambiguous, with disagreement being voiced but, by changing the topics, the individuals never completely addressed or resolved some issues.

For a time, researchers saw these different relationship types as developmental, consistent with interpersonal relationship models. So, for example, the dyad began as strangers (low LMX), but, if the offer to improve the relationship was accepted, the relationship moved to career-oriented acquaintances (middle-group), and then mature relationships (high LMX) (Graen & Uhl-Bien, 1995). However, some research suggests the type of relationship may develop rather quickly to a particular level and then be maintained without further development (Kramer, 1995). So, for example, one individual may develop an overseer relationship that never changes over time and another individual may develop a partnership relationship almost instantly, for a variety of reasons such as common background or "chemistry."

Although research based on an ALS contributed a great deal to understanding the ways that supervisor–subordinate relationships influence organizational members' experiences, the research on LMX provides a more nuanced understanding. Those in high LMX relationships tend to experience the type of participatory, supportive, and open communication with their supervisors that was characterized as effective in the earlier research. Those in low

LMX relationships tend to experience more limited, directive, and closed communication typical of ineffective relationships.

Overall, supervisor–subordinate communication relationships influence new and established employees' adjustment and satisfaction with their organizational membership. Communication with supervisors was the most satisfying organizational source of information for newcomers (Jablin, 1984). Communication associated with high LMX relationships is associated with various positive outcomes including increased satisfaction and commitment, decreased turnover, as well as a variety of individual and group productivity measures (Graen & Uhl-Bien, 1995).

In the scenario, Jordan developed a middle-group relationship with Shanne almost immediately upon joining the organization. This led to inclusion in some decisions and a friendly, personal relationship. Although the relationship never seemed to develop into a high LMX relationship, this positive supervisor relationship contributed to Jordan's workplace commitment and satisfaction.

Peer relationships

Although supervisor–subordinate relationships are a critical component in members' organizational experiences, peer relationships are actually the most common and most available information sources (Louis, Posner, & Powell, 1983). Simply put, in most organizations, members have more peers and communicate with them more frequently than with supervisors.

Peer relationships are viewed as potentially developing along the same lines as interpersonal relationships outside organizations. Peer relationships can potentially grow from acquaintance to friend, from friend to close friend, and from close friend to almost best friend (Sias & Cahill, 1998). The term "almost best friend" was used because many employees, especially men, seemed reluctant to describe workplace relationships as "best friends." The transition to friend was typically associated with proximity and time spent together on work-related activities that provided common ground, along with extra-organizational socializing.

The transition to close friend resulted from communicating about work experiences and family problems more openly and less cautiously. The transition to almost best friend came about through the passage of time and more open communication about various life and work-related events.

Like supervisor–subordinate relationships, it is important to note that not all peer relationships move toward greater intimacy. Kram and Isabella (1985) distinguished between three types of peer relationships. Information peers primarily provide work-related information and discuss superficial topics such as weather or sports. This category seems to characterize acquaintance and beginning friend relationships. Collegial peers provide additional emotional and career support and might be classified as close friends. Special or close peers are the most open and intimate peers. They keep few secrets from each other as they discuss work and family issues and support each other. These represent almost best friends or best friends.

Given the frequency of peer interactions, it is not surprising that peer relationships have important implications for organizational socialization. For example, research on newcomers indicates that communication with peers has an immediate impact on employees' adjustment to organizational settings (Ostroff & Kozlowski, 1992). Newcomers who gained more information from peers were more satisfied, performed better, and were less likely to consider leaving (Morrison, 1993b). Similarly, transferees who received more social support and feedback from their peers generally adjusted more positively to their new jobs by experiencing less stress and role ambiguity along with more satisfaction and job knowledge (Kramer, 1996).

These positive outcomes related to peer communication are probably associated with the types of relationships individuals develop, as suggested in previous typologies. So, for example, individuals who develop more close friends and collegial peers likely receive more feedback and social support from their peers for work and family issues. Those who develop few relationships beyond the acquaintance-information peer level likely feel less supported and as a result are less satisfied and more likely to leave.

Supportive of this interpretation, Zorn and Gregory (2005) found that the friendships that first year medical students developed provided important tangible support in learning their roles, along with socio-emotional support even though they considered those relationships "not yet close."

Interaction between supervisor and peer relationships

Whereas the discussion so far has examined them in isolation, research suggests that there is an interaction between supervisor relationships and peer relationships. In particular, the type of LMX relationship an individual has and the reason for it influences peer relationships. Sias and Jablin (1995) found that peers talked to each other about the nature of relationships between various peers and their supervisors. If a peer had a particularly close (high LMX) supervisor relationship, the others needed to make sense of this. When they perceived the peer as deserving the close relationship because he/she was hard-working and competent, they viewed him/her as a possible communication conduit for influencing the supervisor, but if they perceived the peer as undeserving and simply a brown-nosing subordinate undeserving of special treatment, they tended to isolate and withdraw from the individual. If a peer had a particularly closed (low LMX) relationship with a supervisor, they also made differential sense of it. If the peer deserved the poor relationship because he/she was a poor worker or a negative influence, they maintained their distance from the peer to avoid being associated with him/her, but if they perceived the peer as undeserving of the treatment, as being picked on by the supervisor, they tended to rally around him/her and offer support. So clearly the type of hierarchical relationship between a supervisor and subordinate influences peer relationships.

Peer relationships are the most available sources of organizational socialization. Peers are an important ongoing source of information for managing uncertainty and making sense of organizational experiences. Peers are a source of information for interpreting one's own and other supervisor–subordinate relationships and impact individual outcomes like satisfaction, commitment, and turnover.

In the scenario, Jordan's peer relationships seem to fit the close friend or collegial relationship categories. These supportive peer relationships were part of an overall favorable work environment that contributed to Jordan's positive work attitudes. In addition, peers recognized that Kasey had an insider relationship with their supervisor. Because that relationship was seen as deserving, the peers used Kasey as a conduit for information and influence with Shanne.

Collective workgroup

The discussion of peers so far has treated them either as individuals (one on one relationships) or as a rather amorphous collective. In many instances, individuals work in peer groups or teams who collectively influence the socialization process. Some of the early management research inadvertently discovered the importance of workgroups. In the Hawthorne studies, the researchers found that workgroups enforced productivity norms (Roethlisberger, 1941). Essentially, that research found that, despite management efforts to increase productivity, group members made sure that everyone produced at about the same level and even compensated for each other when someone had a poor day so that group productivity remained stable. Similarly, steel factory employees expected a certain work ethic of others so that they did not let each other down, even if it meant working while sick (Gibson & Papa, 2000).

While the previous examples of groups enforcing norms might seem counter-productive, in many cases, the influence of group norms is positive. At a Harley-Davidson plant, a wide variety of positive results, including improved productivity and cohesion, occurred after introducing self-managed teams which allowed peers to create group norms by making decisions and managing operations (Chansler, Swamidass, & Cortlandt, 2003). In other situations, peer groups enforcing norms are essential for a safe work environment. In high-reliability settings, like firefighting, mining, and aviation, group norms are essential for preventing mistakes that can result in serious injury or death. For example, the development of trust in each other was critical for firefighters in creating a safe work environment (Myers, 2005). New firefighters who demonstrated a strong desire to join by volunteering, a strong work ethic, and humility gained trust and acceptance from the established firefighters. The strong sense of trust and camaraderie allowed them to maintain safety and productivity in the dangerous situations they faced.

In contrast to these positive outcomes, in other situations work teams can develop norms that become negative or oppressive. Self-managed teams can create norms that serve as concertive control over their members. Concertive control can be more powerful than hierarchical or bureaucratic control because it involves self-enforcement by team members. A study of an electronics firm after the company changed to self-managed teams found that team members eventually developed norms that were more powerful and strict than those of the previous hierarchical management (Barker, 1993). For example, individuals were expected to rearrange schedules to work overtime to meet deadlines and one team posted a public record of the number of tardies and absences with the apparent goal of shaming individuals into improved work habits. It seems unlikely that management would attempt to impose such policies, let alone be allowed to practice them without employees challenging them. Concertive control allowed the practice to continue because group members enforced the norms rather than management. Those who did not accept the group norms either voluntarily left or were removed from the team.

Together, research suggests that, collectively, peers in workgroups or teams powerfully influence newcomers and established employees. Their norms may support or oppose management directives and may control group members' behaviors in either positive or negative ways. Jordan's team appears to have developed productive norms that created a positive and successful team. One norm was the expectation that individuals work overtime as a unit instead of individually. Their unhappiness with Jordan for missing such days did not reach the level of concertive control, but suggests the importance of such norms. Jordan, who as a newcomer closely adhered to that norm, seemed more concerned about the group norm than the supervisor's attitude, even as an experienced employee.

Network relationships

In addition to workgroup relationships, part of the socialization process is the development of a network of relationships throughout the organization. These network links may be part of the organization's formal hierarchy and structure or they may emerge informally. Network links provide resources and information to members. A number of different content or topic networks have been identified in organizations, including the following: a task network which assists in getting work done; a social network which provides friendship relationships; an authority network which delineates who has responsibility and reward or punishment power; an innovation network which promotes new ideas and opportunities; and a political network which formally or informally influences the organization's resource allocations (O'Reilly & Roberts, 1977; Tushman, 1977a, 1977b). Some network links provide organizational members with only one type of information or resource and are known as uniplex relationships, while others provide multiple types of information and resources and are known as multiplex relationships.

Network relationships, which range from acquaintance to almost best friend, are important communication resources for organizational members. They are associated with a wide range of positive outcomes including improved employee effectiveness and efficiency, positive work attitudes and behaviors, shared interpretations of organizational structures and personnel, and social support for managing stress (Monge & Contractor, 2001).

Findings like these suggest the importance of network contacts for newcomers and established members.

In some cases, the mere opportunity for network contacts is as important as the specific resources gained. For example, a study of inside bank tellers who had routine contact with a variety of other organizational members throughout their day and of outside tellers who were isolated in toll-booth-like units found that the outside tellers were less satisfied with policies, pay, and management, and had a higher turnover rate (McLaughlin & Cheatham, 1977). The lack of opportunity to network with others in the bank created a range of problems despite all the tellers having the same managers, policies, and so forth. Given these results, it is not surprising that banks switched to group windows with pneumatic tubes for outside tellers for interactions with customers, rather than toll-booths.

The importance of network links is not quite so simple, however. Their importance depends on other individual characteristics. People with high job involvement truly enjoy their work and strongly identify with their jobs while those with low job involvement are not so inclined. A study of employees at a research and development firm found that those with high job involvement did not need communication network involvement in order to be committed to their organizations whereas those with low job involvement needed communication network involvement in order to stay committed (Eisenberg, Monge, & Miller, 1983). This suggests that social relationships in the network led to commitment for those with low job involvement but were unimportant to those with high job involvement.

Overall, network relationships provide a range of resources to organizational members and impact individual (e.g., employee effectiveness and work attitudes) and organizational (e.g., innovation and coordination) outcomes (Monge & Contractor, 2001). In the scenario, Jordan developed a number of network contacts that made doing the job easier and included some social contacts for nonwork activities. As such, network relationships, although perhaps less personal than workgroup relationships, were an important part of the initial and ongoing socialization process.

Mentor relationships

Another important individual relationship in organizational set-tings can be the mentor–protégé relationship. In research, a mentor is typically defined as someone who is of higher status and more experienced than the protégé but who is not in a direct supervisory relationship. By such definitions, a mentor should be in a differ-ent department or part of the organization from the protégé. In common vernacular, this distinction is not always maintained as individuals will talk about the mentoring they received from direct supervisors or peers. Mentors provide a wide range of career and psychosocial benefits for protégés (Kram, 1983). Career benefits include sponsorship for organizational activities, exposure and vis-ibility to influence organizational members, coaching on managing work duties, and help gaining challenging assignments necessary for career advancement. Psychosocial benefits include role mod-eling of appropriate organizational behaviors, feedback to assist in acceptance and confirmation, counseling on dealing with work issues including balancing work, family-time, and friendships.

Like other relationships, mentoring relationships may move through a series of phases (Kram, 1983). The *initiation phase*, which may last 6–12 months, begins with high positive expecta-tions for both individuals. Mentors expect protégés to have high potential and excel in their careers; protégés expect mentors to be influential due to exceptional abilities. The *cultivation phase*, which may last 2–5 years, involves more realistic expectations of each other, but leads to protégés feeling competent and sat-isfied with mentors and the mentors developing confidence in protégés and satisfaction in their role in assisting in the protégés' development.

Eventually a *separation phase* begins. Here the relationships become less central to the protégés. This can be due to various reasons, such as changes in physical locations or protégés devel-oping separate identities or careers. This separation can lead to turmoil, anxiety, or feeling of loss for one or both parties in the relationship. The individuals may either come to accept this change or attempt to return to the previous type of relationship.

The final phase, the *redefinition phase*, involves new relational expectations. Often friendship develops since the individuals are on more equal footing. Protégés have gained experience and may be mentoring newer organizational members. In some cases mentors and protégés are in positions of equal status in different parts of the organization. This can create a number of difficulties and ambiguities as protégés may still want to look up to mentors and mentors may fear being passed over by protégés.

This phase model of mentoring has a number of limitations. First, it should be apparent that not all mentoring relationships follow this pattern. In many instances, particularly when mentors are assigned, relationships never develop beyond initiation and the benefits are limited or nonexistent. In other cases, the relationship may develop very quickly. More importantly, sometimes the relationships that develop have negative rather than positive consequences (Kram, 1983). For example, sometimes mentors hold protégés back rather than assisting them in career development. This may be unintentional, such as when mentors fail to support protégés for a promotion because they think they are not ready yet, without considering that they may be more prepared than other candidates. In other cases, it may be the result of jealousy of the protégés' talents or fear that they may move ahead of the mentors. So mentor relations are typically positive, but can have negative consequences.

Despite concerns over possible negative results, research has consistently demonstrated that mentor relationships are generally positive. Two types of mentoring relationships have been examined, formal and informal. Formal mentoring relationships involve individuals being matched to appropriate experienced mentors as part of an organizational program. Protégés may or may not have input into the selection process. Jablin (2001) concluded that newcomers involved in formal mentoring programs experience a number of important benefits compared to those without mentors, including better understanding of organizational issues and higher satisfaction.

Informal mentoring relationships occur when protégés and mentors develop relationships outside of any official organizational program. As such, they occur naturally based on common interests and mutual trust. A study of mentors in a large health care organization found that individuals in voluntary mentor relationships rated themselves as having more mobility and opportunities, feeling more satisfied, and receiving more recognition, and promotions than those without mentors (Fagenson, 1989). Those in higher positions perceived even more positive outcomes than those in lower-level positions.

Comparisons of formal and informal mentoring generally find that informal mentoring is more advantageous. In a typical study, a comparison of informal, formal, and no mentoring relationships found that those in informal mentoring relationships did the best on a variety of outcomes (Chao, Walz, & Gardner, 1992). Those with informal mentoring reported significantly higher levels of psychosocial and career functions, including more career support along with higher job satisfaction and salaries, than those without mentoring relationships. Those with formal mentoring were generally somewhere between the other two. Similarly, Ragins and Cotton (1999) found that, in addition to more satisfaction and greater compensation, those in informal mentoring relationships reported receiving more career development assistance, including sponsoring, coaching, exposure, and challenging assignments, as well as more psychosocial assistance, including friendship, social support, acceptance, and role modeling, than those in formal relationships. The advantage of informal mentoring may be a combination of the relationship being voluntary rather than forced and of protégés being more selective in choosing top performers as mentors.

A common concern with mentoring is that it may not be equally available or effective for everyone. It can be particularly difficult for women, minorities, or other under-represented groups to find appropriate mentors to serve as role models since there may be an insufficient number of advanced personnel who match their demographics and career aspirations. This is not to say that mentors must have matching demographics to be effective. However, the gender composition of mentoring relationships does impact the outcomes of mentoring in a complex way (Ragins &

Cotton, 1999). Likewise, similarity, including racial similarity, affects the positive outcomes of mentoring (Ensher & Murphy, 1997). Findings like these suggest that mentoring does not benefit everyone equally.

So far the discussion of mentoring has focused on the advantages for protégés who are newcomers. When considering mentoring, it is important to recognize that mentors also may benefit from their roles. Mentoring can groom established members (mentors) for organizational advancement as well (Jablin, 2001). By assisting protégés, mentors demonstrate their organizational knowledge and interpersonal skills, which may be prerequisites to opportunities for their own career advancement. They also may receive satisfaction from assisting their protégés. Thus, while research has generally focused on the value of mentoring for protégés, the mentors receive benefits as well, as part of their ongoing socialization.

In the scenario, Jordan does not appear to have a formal or informal mentor. Some of the information or advice given by Shanne or by contacts in another department perhaps provided mentoring-type information, but no one seems to have assumed a mentoring role. It is difficult to speculate what the impact of a mentor might have been. Perhaps Jordan would have received higher evaluations, raises, or even a promotion as a result of having a mentor.

Differences in organizational relationships

Due to various factors such as gender, race, social class, sexual preferences, abilities, and age, some individuals may not have the same opportunities to develop workplace relationships (Allen, 2004). For example, communication network contacts of minority group members differ from those of the majority group (Ibarra, 1995). Similarly, opportunities for developing positive mentor relationships and outcomes are not the same for men and women (Ragins & Cotton, 1999). As a result, individuals who differ from the organization's majority often feel isolated, due to simultaneously feeling invisible when they are stereotyped, marginalized, or ignored, and overvisible when they receive extra attention for breaking a norm or are expected to represent their demographic group (Dougherty & Krone, 2000). Factors like these negatively affect their ability to develop the same types of peer and supervisor relationships as others.

Difficult relationships

The previous sections suggest mostly positive, or at least cordial, workplace relationships. Unfortunately, a wide range of troublesome relationships often develop in the workplace. These can include problematic supervisors such as self-centered taskmasters and intrusive harassers, peers who are mildly annoying or abrasive and incompetent, or subordinates such as incompetent renegades or abrasive harassers (Fritz, 2006). Many of these workplace relationships are not voluntary relationships. Individuals frequently must maintain workplace relationships with individuals they either would not choose to work with or simply do not like for various reasons. The energy individuals spend managing these unpleasant relationships affects the whole unit's productivity and can lead to stress, dissatisfaction, and even turnover (Fritz, 1997).

Unpleasant relationships

Researchers have examined the strategies individuals use to manage these difficult relationships. One approach classifies the responses along two dimensions: active versus passive and constructive versus destructive (Rusbult & Zembrodt, 1983). An active, constructive approach involves directly addressing the problem to solve it. A passive, constructive approach involves waiting for things to improve, which may or may not happen. An active, destructive approach involves exit, such as moving to a different organizational location or leaving the organization. A passive, destructive approach simply neglects the relationship and allows it to deteriorate.

Taking a different approach, Hess (2000) identified five general strategies that individuals use to maintain relationships with disliked others in nonvoluntary relationships. One strategy involves ignoring the individual and, in effect, dehumanizing them. In this strategy, the disliked other becomes almost a nonperson. A second strategy involves detaching psychologically from the person. This involves changing an attitude toward the person so that what he/she does no longer has an effect. A third strategy is to reduce involvement with the person. This might include no longer working together on projects and avoiding work and social interactions. Depersonalizing the interactions is a fourth strategy. Here an individual no longer views the negative interactions as personal. The final strategy involves showing antagonism toward the person. This would hopefully cause the other person to avoid interactions. Through these various distancing behaviors, individuals manage many of their difficult relationships.

Abusive relationships

Although most employees might accept that they are going to have some unpleasant work relationships that must be managed through distancing behaviors, some workplace relationships move beyond difficult to abusive relationships. One type of abusive relationship is *bullying behavior*. Bullying behavior is defined as a pattern of repeated hostile communication and/or behaviors that are perceived as efforts to harm or control others or even drive them from the workplace (Lutgen-Sandvik, 2006). Much more than simply unpleasant work interactions, bullying involves behaviors like yelling and screaming, throwing papers, and intimidation by invading personal space. The strategies that individuals use to respond to bullying behavior overlap with those used to increase distance from unpleasant work relationships, but include a variety of other options.

Lutgen-Sandvik (2006) identified five broad categories of responses to bullying. One strategy is *confrontation*, either directly or through use of humor in public, to attempt to change the bullying behavior. Unfortunately, sometimes confrontation leads to an escalation of bullying rather than a decrease. *Exodus* through transfers or quitting is another strategy. Unfortunately, this may simply result in the bully directing his/her inappropriate behaviors toward another workgroup member rather than in it subsiding. *Collective voice* involves workgroup members coming together to assist the individual who is being bullied, either by supporting the individual's understanding of the situation, taking action to protect the individual, or collectively voicing their viewpoints. These approaches amount to variations on a "safety in numbers" strategy. *Reverse discourse* involves a variety of communication strategies from documentation and filing grievances, to creating relationships with powerful allies, to embracing the pejorative labels. An example of the last would be claiming that being the troublemaker one is accused of being by the bully is a good thing for the department since change is needed. The final broad category, *subversive (dis)obedience*, includes behaviors like withdrawing from work, over-adhering to work rules to slow down the work, withholding information, or discussing retaliation, although not necessarily carrying it out.

Another type of abusive workplace interaction involves *sexual harassment behaviors*. Although sexual harassment has been legally defined and is prohibited in the USA by federal laws, it is a common experience, with around 13,000 cases filed with the EEOC each year, including 15 percent filed by men (US EEOC, 2008). Estimates suggest 30–70 percent of women experience sexual harassment at some time in their careers, depending on the occupation; similar numbers are reported for female students and faculty members (Wood, 1992). According to the EEOC, sexual harassment can be committed by supervisors, co-workers, or even non-employees. It includes individual acts such as quid-pro-quo, in which sexual favors are requested as necessary to secure employment opportunities, or general activities that create hostile work environments.

It is impossible to identify all of the ways that sexual harassment harms individuals. A series of narratives in a special issue of the *Journal of Applied Communication* (Our stories, 1992) includes a wide range of responses from targets and observers of sexual harassment. A few of these responses are feelings of embarrassment, anxiety, degradation, and devastation. Others experience a loss of trust in co-workers, authority figures, and their occupational setting. Many feel isolated, especially when co-workers, both male and female, do not seem to believe the abusive behaviors occurred, question the target's interpretation of the events, or insinuate that the target encouraged the behaviors. Given these responses, it is not surprising that many targets do not report sexual harassment, or choose to move to different organizations.

Because sexual harassment typically occurs in personal interactions between a predator and target(s), targets use many of the same strategies to cope as do recipients of bullying behaviors. The narratives (Our stories, 1992) provide examples of many of the same strategies, from confrontation to exit. Despite this individual focus, it is important to recognize that sexual harassment incidents have broader relational implications for the entire workgroup. A target is likely to withdraw if the accuracy of a harassment accusation is questioned, but a supportive response from peers and supervisors can lead to less negative outcomes. An analysis of sexual harassment by an organizational guest found that support for the targets by other department members, including demonizing the harasser, greatly reduced the harassment's negative effect (Dougherty & Smythe, 2004). This supportive response was in sharp contrast to the lack of support many targets anticipate when they expect that they will not be believed. Because the perpetrator was an organizational guest, he was easily removed from the setting. Removing sexual harassers can be much more challenging in employment settings, even when policies are in place. However, much in the same way workgroup members can support targets of bullies, supportive responses from co-workers and supervisors creates a culture that rejects harassing behaviors rather than accepting them.

Not all workplace relationships are positive or even neutral as part of the ongoing socialization experience. Unpleasant relationships can range from mildly annoying to bullying or sexually harassing behaviors. In response to negative interactions, individuals develop a variety of coping strategies that range from ignoring to confronting to exiting. Given that workplace relationships influence various employee reactions to work, from commitment to satisfaction and turnover, these negative relationships and the ways individuals respond to them are unfortunate parts of the socialization process. Supportive responses from workgroup members reduce the negative impact of these interactions. In the scenario, Jesse's behaviors probably reached the level of bullying behavior, particularly when requesting individuals be fired for incompetence. To cope with this, the workgroup avoided interaction to the degree possible and the supervisor and peers supported those who were targets of bullying. These coping strategies seemed to prevent Jordan and the others from considering leaving the organization, but nonetheless these bullying behaviors had a negative impact on the workplace environment.

Volunteer organizations

Organizational relationships are at least as important for volunteers as they are for employees. In addition to a commitment to organizational activities or mission, one main reason individuals volunteer is to develop relationships. For example, the two most common reasons members reported for joining a community theater group were to have the opportunity to perform and to develop friendships (Kramer, 2005). Not surprisingly, communication with leadership, along with peer support and interaction, were the best predictors of the community theater members' satisfaction and commitment. This suggests developing positive supervisor and peer relationships is probably vital for volunteers' continued membership.

A number of factors likely make these relationships different for volunteers. In some instances volunteers' supervisors will be paid employees of the organization, giving them some additional status and influence. In other instances, supervisors are also volunteers giving them even less influence. Either way, supervisors have minimal ability to provide rewards or sanctions. Perhaps they can give more desirable assignments to favored volunteers or make sure they are recognized at annual banquets. However, whereas employees may be satisfied to make sense of preferential treatment of their peers, blatant favoritism will probably cause other volunteers to leave. Together this suggests that supervisors of volunteers have limited ability to provide rewards, need to meet volunteers' need for social relationships, and must appear fair and equitable. As such, supervisors of volunteers likely need to work at developing middle to high LMX relationships with volunteers if they wish to retain them.

Volunteer peer relationships range from information peers/acquaintances to close/best friends. What probably differs is that volunteers can actively recruit friends to join with a much greater ease than they can in employment settings. So, whereas employees typically develop friendships after joining an organization, volunteers sometimes enter organizations with a network of friends already developed. Of course, others join without knowing anyone and must develop new friendships. The pre-existence of friendships or the development of friendships influences volunteers' satisfaction and commitment (Kramer, 2005).

Unpleasant relationships likely have an even more negative impact on volunteers than on employees. Whereas employee relationships are nonvoluntary in most instances unless an individual is willing to quit, for volunteers the relationships to the organization and to other members are completely voluntary. As a result, difficult relationships are likely to lead to exit more quickly for volunteers. Exiting has few negative consequences for volunteers, particularly if there are other opportunities to do the same activities in another organization.

The context of some volunteer organizations may change the interpretation of certain behaviors that would be deemed unacceptable in other settings. Kramer (2002) found that communication laced with sexual connotation was common in one community theater group. These behaviors, which would potentially be considered sexual harassment in an employment setting, were part of the fun and playful aspects of participation in the group. So while unpleasant relationships may lead to quick exit for volunteers, what is defined as unpleasant may be quite different from in other contexts.

Finally, success in recruiting and retaining volunteers is influenced by many factors beyond the control of the volunteer organization. Because the relationships are voluntary, they most often do not have the same importance as work and family associations and organizations typically have one-third of their volunteers quit each year (Corporation for National & Community Service, 2007). When time conflicts occur between the three, individuals are most likely to leave the voluntary associations first, even if they have positive relationships with other volunteers.

In the scenario, Jordan joined a runners' club at the encouragement of some work acquaintances. Having a couple of casual friends likely made joining the volunteer club easier. Continued friendship and meeting exercise goals will probably keep Jordan active in the club unless work and family make it difficult to participate.

Conclusions

Interpersonal relationships are an important part of the initial and ongoing socialization process. Through these relationships, individuals acquire knowledge and resources for completing their jobs and develop social relationships that affect their desire to maintain organizational memberships.

7

Transitions

It had been a year of change. Jamie began the year in a start-up software company in Chicago, working with workgroup members like Taylor. When the company expanded, Jamie was selected to lead a new product development group called Irata. The promotion occurred without much formality; the owners called Jamie in one day unexpectedly and offered the position. They indicated that Taylor would be assigned to work for Jamie in Irata as another experienced member, but everyone else would be newcomers.

By imitating others, Jamie did not have much trouble managing the newcomers, despite receiving no training on supervising. Managing Taylor was more problematic. Since they had been co-workers and friends, Jamie found it difficult to treat Taylor as a subordinate, but instinctively knew that it was important to create some distance between them so that other group members would believe they were being treated fairly.

The problem became more severe when the owners told Jamie that the organization was being sold to a West Coast company. Jamie wanted to tell Taylor about this because of its potential impact on jobs, but doing so would break a management confidence. Before Jamie had a chance to say anything, the acquisition was announced at a company-wide meeting. Taylor gave Jamie an inquisitive look, but Jamie acted as if it was a surprise.

After the acquisition announcement, employees were anxious about their status. Jamie was unable to provide much information because management was fairly close-lipped about everything. This seemed to lead to lost productivity as employees frequently talked to each other rather than working. Management directives to get to work simply caused employees to email and text-message instead of talking face-to-face. Taylor occasionally approached Jamie for additional information, but there was none.

At a second company-wide meeting a month after the acquisition announcement, the "other shoe" dropped. The previous owners sat while the new owners announced that they were offering a few people transfers to their West Coast headquarters, but letting the rest go. The lists of those being offered transfers would be out the next day. Of course, no one worked the remainder of that day as they discussed best, worst, and most likely scenarios.

As a manager, Jamie got to see the entire list the next day. Management eliminated everyone else from Irata, including Taylor, but offered Jamie a transfer. Jamie was grateful that the new management team handed out the pink slips.

When Taylor came to talk, Jamie could not say much except that there were plenty of opportunities for someone with Taylor's talents. When Taylor asked if Jamie was going to accept the transfer, the reply was yes. It was their last personal interaction. The company sponsored a party the day before the doors closed. None of those let go were present; they were either using their remaining vacation days or already had new jobs. Jamie and those transferring tried to be upbeat, but it seemed more like a funeral than a party.

Three months later, Jamie was at the company's head-quarters supervising a product development team that was working on a program almost identical to what Irata had been working on. Thinking about Taylor and the others in Chicago made Jamie feel a bit guilty. It would have been nice if someone had explained the personnel decisions.

At one time, our image of employees was of people who went to work for a company after finishing their education, received some promotions during their careers, and then retired from that company, which had not changed much. This image was always more imaginary than real. Although the pace of change has increased, the cliché "the only thing constant is change" has described organizations for decades, even centuries. People likely stayed with the same organizations longer than they do now, but not necessarily their entire careers, and organizations changed due to new personnel, technologies, and attitudes.

Changes of any type, even minor ones, have unforeseen consequences. Recently, we moved the faculty mailboxes from one wall to another to improve office appearance and efficiency. As a consequence, faculty now have to enter the office to check their mail instead of being able to look through the glass door. This minor change increased faculty and staff interactions which may result in other changes. Changes, even small ones, potentially alter an organization's artifacts and rituals, which may modify the organization's culture in small or large ways.

Not everyone responds to changes the same. Some individuals embrace change; others respond negatively to it. The first time I read Deal's (1985) chapter on cultural change, I was astonished to consider that some individuals experience organizational changes with the same intensity that is associated with the loss of loved ones. He suggested that, in response to cultural changes, some individuals go through the five stages of grieving: denial, anger, depression, bargaining, and acceptance. The example used to illustrate this involved a technology change, replacing typewriters with computers in a newsroom. The expected improvements in efficiency were not achieved until a ceremony allowed the employees to mourn the loss of a cultural artifact, their old typewriters.

This chapter considers some of the changes that organizational members experience as part of the ongoing metamorphosis, or change and acquisition, phase of the socialization process. To organize these changes, they are divided into individual transitions and organizational transitions. In keeping with a systemic view of change, it is important to consider how individual changes influence the broader workgroup and to consider how organization-wide changes influence individuals.

Individual transitions

Because socialization is ongoing, individuals are constantly in a state of change as part of their role negotiation process. Rather than focus on these constant changes, this section focuses on three common individual transitions. The first two clearly are career transitions: job promotions and job transfers. The third, reaching a career plateau, is also a career transition although it may not involve changing jobs.

Job promotions

Although one of the most common employee transitions with critical implications for the individuals involved and their organizations, surprisingly, job promotions receive little scholarly attention (Hill, 2003). Scholars have been more interested in CEO successions than in the promotion of those lower in the hierarchy to positions as managers and supervisors. Job promotions most often occur in response to other leadership changes. These personnel changes may be planned (known in advance) or unplanned (someone unexpectedly leaves). They can be for a variety of reasons such as retirements, voluntary resignations or firings, along with promotions, transfers, or lateral moves of previous leaders.

Experiencing a promotion It is easy to consider the experiences of individuals being promoted as a significant change that is part of the ongoing socialization process. The promotion process has been described as a series of stages similar to the stages of socialization: pre-promotion, shifting, and adjustment (Kramer & Noland, 1999). The *pre-promotion phase* occurs from the time there is a possible opening until it is filled, which can vary significantly depending on whether the change was planned or unplanned. During this time, individuals attempt to demonstrate that they are qualified for the promotion based on factors like work experience, quality of work, and educational background. Either the individuals or their managers may initiate the process of being considered for the promotion. Individuals who are being groomed for promotions may automatically be considered. Individuals who may be missing some prerequisite background, for example a college degree or particular work experience, may be overlooked unless they make a case for why they should be considered despite a deficiency. In some cases, the interview may be formal, involving several levels of managers or participation in testing centers. In other cases, it may be only a short conversation in which the individuals are asked if they are interested and then told they have the promotion.

The shifting phase involves learning the necessary skills and taking on new responsibilities associated with the promotion. The phase's beginning can be difficult to determine since sometimes responsibilities are added before the promotion's official start date. The shifting involves a variety of role negotiations besides job duties. Former peers often become subordinates; former managers become peers. In addition, the workgroup has expectations for the position based on the person who previously held it. During this time, the promoted individual must gradually develop a new identity as a manager (Hill, 2003).

The start of the *adjustment phase* is also difficult to determine since it probably occurs gradually and is more psychological than time-based. Hill (2003) suggests that new managers must struggle with three main problems in adjusting to their positions: (1) reconciling their expectations with the realities of managing; (2) handling numerous conflicts with and between subordinates; and (3) making sense of the expectations and demands of their subordinates, peers, and superiors. At some point, the promoted individual feels confident and comfortable in the new position after satisfactorily resolving those issues. The job becomes fairly routine, or at least as routine as it can be. The workgroup becomes fairly stable again. Of course, in many organizations, stability never really occurs as turnover occurs in the workgroup or the person prepares for another promotion.

Communication changes. Kramer and Noland (1999) identified important communication changes that occur during promotions. After the promotion, communication changes with former peers. Former peers and confidants may attempt to take advantage of previous relationships. In order to avoid showing favoritism, or due to organizational policy, the promoted individual may need to break those close ties. It can be challenging to get new peers to communicate on an equal basis with their former subordinate. Promoted individuals often have new communication responsibilities including interacting with additional members of management, customers, or vendors. Perhaps the most challenging new communication skill is managing information. In their new positions, they often have access to confidential organizational and personnel information. They most likely have no experience or training for determining when and if to share that information. Many of these communication skills were not important in their previous positions.

Testing or hazing. A surprising finding in the Kramer and Noland (1999) study was the presence of testing or hazing of those recently promoted. Although this may be unique to the restaurant business used in the study, nearly all of their participants reported that they were either tested or hazed in their new positions. Testing was viewed as appropriate behaviors in which subordinates, peers, or supervisors questioned or pushed them to see if they had the necessary job skills. This could be something as simple as knowing the costs or ingredients for menu items. Hazing was viewed as inappropriate behaviors in which others seemed to simply want to see if they could push the right buttons to upset the person. This might include yelling about something over which the person had no control, to see the reaction. The difference between the two was not always clear. Although it is probably less obvious in other settings, it seems likely that those promoted need to prove themselves to those around them as they transition into their new positions.

Experiencing leadership changes. Whereas the previous section focused on the individual being promoted, a more complete perspective also considers workgroup member experiences. A new supervisor/manager/leader changes the workgroup experience as well.

Although research on leadership succession has focused on CEOs, the results seem applicable here. Workgroup members are likely to experience one of the three types of leadership changes: (1) in *heir apparent* successions, an insider who was groomed for the position receives the promotion; (2) in *contender successions*, an insider with ideas that differ from those of the outgoing leader receives the promotion; (3) in *outsider successions*, someone outside the group and most likely outside the organization, is brought in to fill the position (Shen & Cannella, 2002). The differences in these types of successions are important for the workgroup. In the heir apparent succession, because the person was groomed for the position, the workgroup likely expects the work setting to remain fairly unchanged. In the other two types, the expectations are probably that there will be significant changes. By choosing someone different from the departing leader, management signals that they want change; the person promoted is expected to make changes, perhaps to increase productivity or improve morale. Regardless of the type of succession, the workgroup culture changes in subtle or obvious ways.

The workgroup members probably experience phases similar to those for the individual promoted. Ballinger and Schoorman (2007) suggest four phases. *Discovery* is the time when the workgroup finds out that the current leader is leaving. *Exit* is when the leader actually leaves the group. Together these two are like the pre-promotion phase. *Entry* describes the time when the new supervisor assumes the role, like the shifting phase. *Stabilization*, like the adjustment phase, describes the time when the workgroup has adjusted to the new leadership and work becomes more routine.

An important part of the workgroup experience during promotions relates to the type of supervisor–subordinate relation that existed with the outgoing supervisor and the type of succession (Ballinger & Schoorman, 2007). For example, those in high LMX relationships with an outgoing supervisor may have positive reactions to an heir apparent since they may perceive that they will continue to benefit from similar relationships. They may be more concerned about the uncertainty of the changes caused by the other two types of succession. By contrast, those in low LMX relationships may welcome contender and outsider successions since they signal opportunities for changes. If they are unhappy with their low LMX relationships, they may be leery of heir apparent successions as representing business as usual.

Regardless of the type of succession, the workgroup may be quite active in attempting to socialize the new leader. The newly promoted leader may have difficulty socializing the group into new ways of doing things; they may resist the new leader's change initiatives, particularly if they perceive themselves as successful in the past. Even when the new group leader is from within the group, the workgroup members must still re-negotiate their relationships with him/her due to the status changes.

Confounding problem with promotions.   One of the confounding issues with job promotions is that individuals are often promoted because they are good at their current jobs, but they may not have the skills needed to be effective in their new jobs. For example, prior to a promotion an individual likely possesses specific technical or analytical skills that make them good at their jobs; being a good manager involves personnel management skills, the ability to delegate, and other non-technical skills (Hill, 2003). As a result, it is not uncommon for individuals to be promoted to positions for which they lack certain competencies. A cynical take on this, known as the Peter Principle, concludes that individuals tend to rise to their level of incompetency in a hierarchy because they are promoted until they are not good (incompetent) at their job (Peter & Hull, 1969). Although this overgeneralization fails to recognize that individuals can develop new skills, from a socialization perspective it suggests the need to look at factors beyond competence in a current job in considering promotions.

It also suggests the need for skill training for promotions, rather than simply expecting individuals to be able to step in. Those promoted may need the same amounts of training as newcomers are given.

Job transfers

Individual experience. Job transfers are another common individual career transition. These can be as simple as transferring to another department within the same building or transferring across the street or across town to another facility. The focus of the research and discussion here is on geographic transfers in which individuals move to another city to work at a different facility operated by the same company. That city may be across the state, the country, or international boundaries. In a few instances, transfers are a group process when a department or division is moved as part of corporate restructuring (Gross, 1981), but the focus here will be on individual transfers.

Studies by the Employee Relocation Council (Brett & Werbel, 1980) and a series of longitudinal studies by Kramer (1993a, 1993b, 1995, 1996) provide much of the background on job transfers. Similar to promotions, job transfers are conceptualized as occurring in three phases: loosening, transition, and tightening (Kramer, 1989). The *loosening phase* represents the time period from when individuals first consider a job transfer until they leave the old location. This includes the process of deciding whether to apply for and/or accept a transfer, as well as the time between the decision to leave and the actual departure. Either management or individuals may initiate transfers. Motivations for individuals transferring may include career advancement opportunities, a desire for a new work environment, or a desire to live in a different location, perhaps closer to family or friends. Management may initiate transfers for reasons like developing employees, placing key personnel in needed locations, distributing personnel, or solving other personnel issues. Those accepting transfers tend to be younger with less organizational tenure; they have experienced fewer lateral moves and see transfers either as opportunities for career development, or as a way to avoid negative career consequences if they turn them down (Brett & Werbel, 1980).

After accepting the transfer, the individual gradually reduces involvement in the current location by completing or withdrawing from projects, and by not taking on new projects that extend past the departure date. In anticipation of a departure, co-workers may inadvertently reduce communication to transferees as they seek out other sources of information to replace them and may overtly communicate their withdrawal by saying things like, "Oh, you won't be here then anyway." Typically, transferees communicate with future supervisors during this time, although this is quite varied. Future supervisors may choose to keep most of the information until after the transfer is complete to reduce stress and allow the transferee to withdraw from the old location, or may attempt to provide information so the person can be up-to-speed from the start. Most transferees experience some sort of farewell event during the last few days at the old location.

The *transition phase* for transferees is, much like the newcomer experience, filled with stress, uncertainty, and ambiguity. Unlike newcomers, transferees already have knowledge of the general organizational culture, but still need to learn the specific location's subculture. Transfers may involve lateral moves, promotions, and even demotions. This means that transferees must learn their task roles, develop social relationships, and learn the norms and politics of how things get done at the new location.

Communication with supervisors and peers is important during the transition phase, but appears to work somewhat differently from how it does for newcomers. Ostroff and Kozlowski (1992) found that peers had a short-term impact on newcomers' adjustment, but the supervisors had an ongoing influence. Kramer (1995, 1996) found the opposite for transferees. Supervisors' communication during the first month influenced transferees' adjustment throughout the first year, but supervisor communication at three months and a year had limited impact. In contrast, peer communication affected transferees' adjustment throughout the first year. These differences may be related to the tendency for job changers to cope with the stress of their new positions by working long hours and delegating responsibilities, while new-comers are more likely to seek information, feedback, and social support (Feldman & Brett, 1983). Supervisors who provide transferees information during the initial months, even if they do not request it, probably help them to cope, but, if the supervisors miss that opportunity, transferees likely cope through their peer relationships.

As presented, it may appear that the loosening and transition phases are quite distinct from each other. In reality, they often overlap. Sometimes transferees assume responsibilities at new locations prior to leaving old locations. They may travel back and forth completing projects at the old locations while working at the new locations. Changing communication technologies will likely blur the distinction more in the future. Family and nonwork activities may also blur the distinction since transferees average eight weeks waiting for their families to move (Brett, 1982) and so they may not feel as if they have left the previous location during the separation.

Like metamorphosis for newcomers, the *tightening phase* for transferees is probably defined more by psychological adjustment than by time. The tightening phase occurs when transferees feel their new jobs have become fairly routine. The transition is quicker and smoother if transferees are well informed about the new position prior to the move (Brett & Werbel, 1980). Some transferees mention nonwork experiences as important in making this transition. For example, celebrating a major holiday with family and visitors can help to solidify the feeling that they are at home in the new location. Transferees feel better adjusted if their family has also adjusted by developing social contacts in the community.

The tightening phase may be quite temporary for transferees. Although they sometimes stay in their new locations for many years, for others another transfer begins before they are acclimated to their new jobs. At one time, IBM was jokingly referred to as representing "I've Been Moved" due to the frequency of transfers. Although, certainly, the economic climate influences the number of transfers in any given year, in many large organizations job transfers are a common careers experience.

International transfers. The goal of international transfers is usually employee development. Employees exposed to facilities in other countries, usually for a fixed period of time, have a broader organizational knowledge than those who only work in one location or country. International transfers add additional uncertainty and complexity which suggests individuals must be carefully selected and prepared (Mendenhall & Oddou, 1985). International transferees face additional problems learning the international location's culture and often the language. Adjustment for family members is often more difficult due to cultural differences and trailing spouses' inability to work. Frequently, adjustment problems for themselves and their families are sufficiently severe for them to return prior to the completion of the expected term. Then these expatriates, as they are often called, face the adjustment of returning to their home country, often to another new location, with the added concern of how being unsuccessful will influence their careers.

Influence on others. The previous sections focused on job transferees' experiences. It is important to recognize that the individual transferring influences the ongoing socialization of two employee groups as well: those remaining at the old location and those at the new location. Kramer (1989) identified at least four potential impacts on those remaining. First, other organizational members must make sense of their colleague's departure. This includes those in the immediate workgroup, but can also involve network links throughout the organization. These individuals want to know reasons for the transfer, such as whether it is indicative of some larger organizational issue or simply a personal preference or opportunity. Second, in most instances, co-workers who are friends participate in some sort of farewell event, much like a retirement event. The length of service and number of friends affects the size and scope of such events. These may range from a last lunch together to a celebration with gifts and speeches. Next, after the individual transfers, co-workers must rebuild their task and social networks. In some cases, the transferee is not replaced and work must be reallocated. Even if there is a replacement, the group must adjust to the replacement's work habits and personality. Finally, a co-worker's transfer can be the catalyst for others to evaluate their own careers. After making sense of their colleague's departure, the remaining co-workers may be motivated to make changes, such as looking at other career options or seeking transfers themselves.

The addition of a transferee into a workgroup is much like the arrival of any other newcomer. The group must adjust to the changes, especially if the transferee is in a leadership position. Transferees are somewhat different from typical newcomers in that they are aware of the general organizational culture and more experienced. As a result, expectations may be higher for transferees, but the workgroup still must accommodate and adjust to the changes, another career transition for them. In organizations that rely heavily on transfers for employee development, workgroups may become skilled at adjusting to the arrival and departure of supervisors and begin to see their role as training new managers.

Career plateaus as individual transitions

The final individual transition to examine is at first glance a non-transition. Most employees eventually reach a career ceiling or peak and become stagnant. Often described as career plateaus, leveling off or stagnating can result from a variety of factors. Some individuals lack the cognitive or behavioral skills to advance further. Since there are fewer positions higher up than at lower levels, not everyone can advance. The move to flatter organizational structures decreases the number of advanced positions available. The presence of a large baby boomer population in the workforce contributes to the problem at this time as well.

Regardless of the cause, individuals who reach a plateau face a transition. It is not a transition in position, but rather a transition of attitude or perspective. After individuals recognize that they have reached a career plateau, they must reassess any expectation of continued career ladder growth and determine their affective, attitudinal, and behavioral response to this (non)event. Not everyone responds to career plateaus the same. Some individuals expect continued promotion throughout their careers while others expect to remain in the same position with little mobility (Hylmo & Buzzanell, 2003).

Research has considered whether career plateaus should be defined objectively, such as by length of time in a position or lack of upward mobility, or subjectively based on a perception that advancement is unlikely or impossible. In comparisons of these two, the subjective plateau was much more significant in predicting attitudes; whereas the objective plateau was not predictive of work-related satisfaction or intention to quit, the subjective plateau was negatively related to satisfaction with the work, supervisor, and organization, along with perceptions of equity in the organization's reward and promotion system (Tremblay, Roger, & Toulouse, 1995). Attribution theory possibly explained these results. When individuals were successful in advancing in the organization, they felt in control and attributed their successes to internal efforts, and were satisfied with their work and believed that policies were equitable. When individuals felt they had stagnated by reaching a plateau, they looked for external explanations and blamed the inequity of the organizational reward system for their situation, and became dissatisfied.

Not all employees who reach a plateau become dissatisfied. Some are pleased that they no longer need to focus on achieving hierarchical status and can pursue other interests. Research indicates that certain coping strategies benefit employees who reach a plateau (Rotondo & Perrewe, 2000). Plateaued and non-plateaued employees use positive coping strategies such as seeking new job assignments, special projects, and mentoring, or by becoming a functional/technical expert. For the plateaued employees these activities were associated with job satisfaction, commitment, and self-reported work effort, but not for non-plateaued employees. This suggests that these behaviors helped plateaued employees to cope with their status. The use of negative coping strategies, such as blaming supervisors or the organization, reporting reductions in the quality and quantity of work effort, or participating in substance abuse were associated with lower satisfaction, commitment, and effort in the plateaued group.

The plateau transition for employees can be a positive or a negative experience. Results like these suggest that communication from supervisors and peers that encourages positive coping with a career plateau can assist employees during this transition. Allowing negative coping strategies likely leads to individuals becoming "deadwood" who hang on until retirement.

Summary of individual transitions

The individual transitions examined here represent three major transitions individuals may experience during a career. Due to biases, some individuals may have different opportunities to experience promotions or transfers. For example, women have typically been under-represented in educational administrative positions, a pattern that is only recently beginning to change. Various testing procedures for determining promotions have been challenged in the courts because they result in under-representation of certain groups in supervisory positions. Perhaps the only equal-opportunity transition is the career plateau; nearly everyone plateaus at some point in their career.

In the scenario, Jamie experienced a promotion and a transfer. The promotion was initiated by management and involved little or no training, a surprisingly common experience. Jamie learned to supervise by imitating others but had difficulty figuring out how to manage a former peer/friend. One of the biggest challenges was managing information, such as the news of the likely acquisition. Then, before getting adjusted to the buy-out, Jamie began another transition with a transfer to the new company's headquarters. It would not be surprising if another individual transition happened before stabilization occurred.

Organizational transitions

It is impossible to attempt to write about all the organizational transitions individuals may experience during their years of employment. There are broad organizational transitions related to organizational life cycles, including birth, growth, maturity, revitalization, and decline (Quinn & Cameron, 1983). The socialization experiences for newcomers and experienced members vary significantly by the life cycle phase. Rather than focus on these global and more gradual changes, this section focuses on two very explicit organizational transitions, mergers and acquisitions, and layoffs or reductions-in-force (RIFs), as representative of organizational changes that occur during employees' metamorphosis experiences.

Mergers and acquisitions (M&As)

During the 1990s M&As occurred at rates of over 20,000 per year, involving $3 trillion in assets (Daniel & Metcalf, 2001), although during economic downturns like those that occurred in the first decade of the twenty-first century, the pace was slower. These numbers suggest that it is not unusual for individuals to experience M&As during their careers. M&As that involve large, publicly traded corporations, like Delta and Northwest Airlines or In Bev and Anheuser-Busch, make national and international news. Many other M&As receive limited media coverage but are equally significant to those involved, such as when a local family-owned rent-to-own company is purchased by a regional competitor, or a local car dealer purchases a competing dealership.

Although technically mergers are between equal partners, members of both organizations rarely view it that way by the process's end. Based on who holds key positions and which systems and processes dominate the combined company, there is usually a sense that an acquisition occurred in which one organization gained control over the other. For example, during a merger between a bank and a leasing company, members of the leasing company originally referred to it as a merger, but eventually called it a take-over; those in the bank always viewed it as an acquisition (Bastien, 1992). In other instances, everyone knows it was an acquisition involving unequal partners. This may be viewed positively or negatively depending on the acquired organization's financial status.

It is useful to consider M&As according to a timeline or phases: pre-merger, in-play, transition, and stabilization (Napier, Simmons, & Stratton, 1989). The first period, the *pre-merger phase*, involves negotiations which may be secret or public. Recommendations to keep negotiations secret suggest that doing so maintains employee productivity and avoids embarrassment if negotiations fail. Recommendations for being open about holding negotiations suggest that this allows for some rumor control since employees inevitably become suspicious or are aware prior to official announcements. Frequently employees and stakeholders report having heard before any official statements, suggesting that rumors are common even if negotiations are kept secret.

The *in-play phase* refers to the time between the formal announcement and the merger actually taking place. This is a time of high uncertainty for members of both organizations, but particularly for those in the acquired organization (Napier et al., 1989). Individuals experience job uncertainty since layoffs are common during M&As. More broadly, they are uncertain how culture differences that exist will affect their work as new procedures and policies go into place. Mixed messages are also common during this time. Organizational spokespersons tell financial stakeholders that they will achieve success, which usually means there will be layoffs, but tell employees that their jobs are secure; when unions are involved, their representatives may also claim jobs are secure, but that employees need the union for job security.

The *transition phase* begins after the merger's legal aspects have been completed and the two organizations begin operating as one. This can involve gradually merging the various organizational systems, including technical systems (information and communication), physical structures (closing or merging facilities), management structures (merging departments or divisions), human resources, and organizational cultures.

A longitudinal study indicated communication's critical role during the in-play and transition phases (Schweiger & DeNisi, 1991). Using two comparable plants involved in the same merger, the researchers and company developed two different communication plans. Communication for the one plant included a realistic merger preview (similar to realistic job previews), weekly department meetings, newsletters with a question-and-answer section, and even a hotline for rumor control. The other plant only received formal announcements about the merger. Although employees at both plants experienced significant increases in uncertainty, stress, and absenteeism, and declines in job satisfaction and commitment, the plant with the multifaceted communication plan had significantly higher levels of trust, job satisfaction, and commitment, along with lower levels of uncertainty, than the other. In fact, because morale was so much lower in the plant with the limited communication plan, the organization ended the experiment and began the multifaceted plan at the second plant.

Merging two cultures can involve much more subtle organizational aspects than systems and structures. For example, the bank/leasing company merger involved a number of important cultural differences (Bastien, 1992). The leasing company was used to making decisions quickly, sealed with handshakes; the bank insisted on detailed contracts approved by several levels of hierarchy. Leasing company employees wore casual clothes while bank employees wore suits. Even the language used to discuss contracts varied between the two organizations. Employees in the acquired leasing company used one of three primary coping strategies. Some simply accommodated the bank's culture and switched to its business suits and language. These individuals tended to receive career advancements. Some practiced code switching in which they communicated differently depending on their audience. These individuals tended to leave the organization over time. The third group resisted the bank's culture on the premise that they needed to maintain the leasing company culture in order to work with their customer base. These individuals tended to remain in the leasing location where the staff became smaller.

The communication needs differ for those in the acquired and acquiring organizations. Employees in acquired organizations primarily are concerned about job security and job duties, while those in acquiring organizations are more concerned about company changes (Zhu, May, & Rosenfeld, 2004). It also appears that the quality of the information, the tone of the communication (positive versus arrogant), and symbolic statements like promoting individuals from the acquired organization into important positions, rather than the quantity of communication, help those in the acquired organization to adjust (Cornett-DeVito & Friedman, 1995). Of course, providing accurate information to reduce uncertainty will not always lead to increased satisfaction and commitment after an acquisition. Initially, pilots of an acquired airline were pleased with the acquisition because of their company's financial difficulties; however, when they became certain that they would lose their seniority in the acquiring airline, they were less positive about the acquisition (Kramer, Dougherty, & Pierce, 2004).

The *stabilization phase* is conceptualized as the time when the new, combined organization has reached a business-as-usual attitude and a unified culture. This may be more imaginary than real. For example, years after an acquisition by a larger airline, employees of the acquired company continued to have annual picnics and participated in other symbolic activities (e.g. secretly having tattoos of this old company's logo) that maintained a distinct subculture (Pierce & Dougherty, 2002). The stabilization phase also may be an illusion because additional organizational changes may occur before stabilization occurs. For example, there may be additional acquisitions, or the organization may determine that it needs to enact reductions-in-force in order to achieve its goals.

M&As are common organizational experiences. Prior experience with mergers and similarities in culture and operating systems seem to increase the success rate, but most evidence suggests that approximately 75 percent of M&As fail to achieve their financial and strategic goals (Kramer et al., 2004). As a result, M&As are often followed by reductions-in-force even if they were not originally planned.

Layoffs or reductions-in-force (RIFs)

Whereas M&As are viewed positively by one or both of the organizations, layoffs or RIFs are rarely viewed that way. Given the negative connotation for individuals who lose their jobs, it is not surprising that a number of euphemisms have been created, including human resource reallocation, streamlining, and right-sizing instead of downsizing. RIFs become necessary when demand for an organization's products or services is significantly smaller than its capacity. This mismatch can result from many factors, including poor strategic planning, failed M&As, or sudden, unexpected environmental changes.

When RIFs do not involve a large percentage of the organization's personnel, they are often accomplished without actually dismissing employees. An organization can reduce its workforce through natural attrition with a hiring freeze, through early retirement incentive plans, or through transfers to other organizational departments or facilities. Being a victim or survivor of an RIF is a common part of many individuals' careers, since they occur in some organizations even in the best of economic times, but are common during economic downturns.

Like M&As, it is useful to think of RIFs as occurring in phases over time. During the *pre-announcement phase*, employees exchange rumors in response to the uncertainty they experience as they see diminishing amounts of work, see managers and upper management holding secret meetings, or hear bad economic news concerning the company. Individuals may consider or actively pursue job alternatives. Time spent making sense of these concerns may result in productivity loss.

There is often a *general announcement*, where employees are notified of general layoffs without specific details of exactly who will be affected, followed by *individual announcements* in which individuals are told specifically whether they will or will not be retained. Individual announcements may include severance packages based on tenure, and the organization may offer job search assistance. Limiting the time between the general and individual announcements is likely to be valuable since, during this time, employees experience increases in stress, job insecurity, and intention to leave, along with decreases in morale, productivity, commitment, and job satisfaction. In addition to intention to leave, employees with options may actually pursue and accept employment elsewhere, regardless of whether they will be retained or not.

166

Sometimes, the time between announcements and the actual layoffs can be extensive. In some instances, after the general announcement, employers use performance reviews and skills assessment tests to determine who will be retained or laid-off; after that, the two groups of employees may continue to work side-by-side for long periods of time, even up to 18 months (Tourish, Paulsen, Hobman, & Bordia, 2004). Under those circumstances, survivors have more trust in their managers and colleagues than those laid-off, but both groups have similar levels of uncertainty about their work.

In more typical instances, the time between the announcements and the layoffs is quite brief, perhaps as short as the time it takes to clear out an office of personal artifacts. The communication with survivors is important during the *post-layoff phase*. Since employees feel they lack information, they experience career uncertainty and have an increased propensity to leave the organization; supportive communication from managers and workgroup members can increase work satisfaction and reduce turnover (Johnson, Bernhagen, Miller, & Allen, 1996). Unfortunately, middle managers who need to provide this support often perceive themselves as uninformed (Tourish et al., 2004).

Information deprivation is also associated with changes in employees' information-seeking. Employees tend to reduce overt information requests, most likely out of impression management concerns, and instead increase their use of observation and third-party information-seeking (Casey, Miller, & Johnson, 1997). As a result, they often receive incomplete or inaccurate information. Given employees' reluctance to seek information directly from managers, the general findings for communication during organizational change apply. Providing partial information, even while admitting to an inability to provide more, has a more positive impact on employees than remaining secretive or waiting to share until there is complete information (DiFonzo & Bordia, 1998).

Those who retain their jobs often experience survivor guilt, which may motivate them to work harder, but can also create a sense of futility and decreased productivity depending on factors like their self-esteem and the likelihood of additional layoffs

(Brochner et al., 1993). After a first round of layoffs, survivors continue to feel uncertain because further layoffs are common. Those who were in workgroups that were spared layoffs actually experience more uncertainty than those in workgroups that experienced cuts (Casey et al., 1997). Apparently, they expect that they will be the target of a second round of layoffs, which frequently occurs. Providing additional information appears to be the only viable approach for addressing these concerns.

If the reason for the RIF was a temporary problem, organizations sometimes actually hire back laid-off employees in the future. This is a common cycle in some industries. If the reason is more systemic or long-term, employees must evaluate the merit of staying with the organization. It is not uncommon for there to continue to be a loss of top employees after an RIF as they seek more stable opportunities in other organizations.

Summary of organizational changes

There simply are too many possible organizational changes to explore in a single chapter. The two examined, mergers and acquisitions and reductions-in-force, are representative of the types of changes that affect organizations and their employees. Others would include organizational restructuring (Balogun & Johnson, 2004) or organizational cycles like birth, growth, maturity, decline, and even organizational death (Quinn & Cameron, 1983). Like the two examined here, communication influences the way that employees adapt to these changes.

Organizational transitions frequently have differential effects on people of different backgrounds. For example, since layoffs frequently are based on tenure, those lower in the organization and most recently hired are often laid-off first. In monolithic and plural organizations (Larkey, 1996), this likely means that employees from under-represented groups are let go first. National statistics regularly show that minorities experience higher levels of unemployment than majority members after layoffs during economic downturns.

In the scenario, Jamie felt something like an insider by hearing about the acquisition before others. However, the lack of communication from upper management led to uncertainty and productivity loss among the workgroup. The lack of supportive communication from management similarly made it difficult to make sense of the RIF that followed. More effective communication might have helped Jamie and others to respond more positively to these changes. Jamie may continue to experience high levels of career uncertainty, despite having a current position, and look for employment elsewhere.

Volunteer organizations

The experiences of volunteer membership in organizations are no more stable than those of employees. Volunteers experience individual transitions as they change organizational roles. In some instances they may be elected to supervisory positions, but in other cases may be promoted to lead groups because they have the most experience. Regardless of how they are promoted, they likely receive limited training, especially in small organizations. For example, when I volunteered to switch from parent assistant to coach for my daughter's soccer team, I was required to attend four hours of training. When I was elected president of my local congregation, my "training" consisted entirely of being handed the gavel.

Volunteers sometimes transfer within the larger organization, although it is usually part of a geographic move related to work or family rather than to the volunteer organization. Various national organizations, such as scouting or the Red Cross, allow individuals to transfer their credentials and experience from one location to another. Many religious organizations have formal procedures for transferring members between congregations.

Organization-wide transitions are more often related to growth or decline than to M&A or RIFs. There are exceptions. On rare occasions, two congregations, two social agencies, or two community groups merge. In those instances, the same issues of combining the cultures of the two organizations are problematic.

When volunteer organizations experience declines, they may

lay off paid employees, but are unlikely to dismiss volunteers. However, if programs that interested the volunteer are discontinued, the volunteer may choose to leave.

Conclusions

Transitions are a common part of the ongoing socialization process for individuals in their occupations and volunteer activities. Some transitions are more individual, such as being moved into supervisory positions; others are more organization-wide, such as when two organizations merge. The frequency of such changes emphasizes that socialization is an ongoing process throughout the time individuals participate in organizations, as they continue to negotiate their roles throughout their experiences.

8

Organizational Exit

Avery was having a bad week as manager of Clothing Outlet.
Staff turnover was always problematic in retail, but needing to
replace three workers in one week was too much. Mackenzie
was going home after graduation next weekend as planned;
this job was always just a means to pay bills during college.
Avery had noticed Payton's effort and attitude had slipped
lately suggesting dissatisfaction with work. So that resigna-
tion was not surprising, just abrupt without even two weeks'
notice. Then there was Corey. Avery first spotted problems
with Corey months ago. After working on improving work
habits informally for three months, Avery finally gave Corey
the choice of meeting specific goals or being dismissed.
After documenting the failure to meet those goals, Avery's
remaining tasks today were firing Corey and then attending
Mackenzie's farewell party at the restaurant next door.

Eventually all members leave their organizations for one reason
or another. This final transition in the organizational assimilation
process is referred to as organizational exit, disengagement, or
turnover, among other labels. Under-studied compared to entry,
the available research still provides a framework for examining
exit processes. Specifically, previous research suggests that there
are two dominant forms of exit: voluntary and involuntary. These
are the focus of this chapter. A third form of exit that blurs the
distinction between these two is discussed as well.

171

The distinction between voluntary and involuntary exit is seemingly simple. Voluntary exit occurs when individuals perceive that they make a choice to initiate the process of leaving; involuntary exit occurs when someone else initiates the process of forcing individuals to leave so that they have little or no choice (Bluedorn, 1978). Because the third category of exit blurs this distinction, individuals may disagree on whether a particular exit was voluntary or involuntary.

Voluntary exit

Motivations for voluntary exit

Voluntary exit occurs for a wide variety of reasons. Research by Lee, Mitchell, Wise, and Fireman (1996) suggested four paths to voluntary exit. Each path has different motivations and involves different processes and communication patterns.

Planned exit. Some voluntary exits are planned ahead of time and are often related to nonwork events such as a pregnancy, a spouse's transfer or retirement, or graduation. Because a date can be projected for these events, individuals generally know in advance when they will leave and develop a script or plan to follow.

These individuals typically communicate openly about their upcoming departure with family, supervisors, and co-workers since there is little point in secrecy. Although someone may attempt to talk these individuals out leaving if it is a possibility, most people are supportive and excited for the employees. Because everyone generally has a positive attitude about these changes, it is common to have farewell events or parties to mark their departures.

Shock resulting in quitting. The second path involves some sort of shock that is serious enough to cause the individual to quit immediately. Typically shocks relate to organizational events or actions, such as the discovery of something unethical about the organization, a merger announcement, or being upset by something such as being passed over for a promotion. The shock is significant enough for the individual to quit, perhaps immediately.

The immediate departure limits communication in this situation. The individual may consult with relatives or close friends prior to quitting, although not always. Communication with organizational members likely includes little more than an announcement and perhaps an explanation of the reason for leaving for selected individuals. The abrupt departure limits farewell events.

Shock resulting in a job search before quitting. The primary difference with this path is that the individual first completes a job search prior to quitting. Two factors seem to contribute to choosing this path over the previous one. First, many individuals in Lee et al. (1996) who quit without job searches were nurses. It seems likely that the high demand for nurses and relative ease in finding other positions contributed to their quitting without another job. Thus, when job opportunities are abundant, quitting without a job is common; when opportunities are scarce, a search likely proceeds quitting. Second, the severity of the shock probably influences the choice. Severe shocks, for example a blatant quid-pro-quo sexual harassment request, might lead to quitting without a job search whereas a hostile work environment may lead to a job search before quitting.

Communication in this path is likely to be secretive and limited. The individuals probably only inform a few close friends or relatives that they are conducting job searches and planning to quit. Only when new jobs are secured is the information widely shared as the individuals announce their departures. Also, to avoid burning bridges for future references or employment, the individuals may avoid explicitly discussing the shock and often explain their departures in terms of new opportunities or a need for a change. The time between announcing a departure and actual exit allows for a farewell event.

Gradual disenchantment. For this path, there is no particular event that motivates exit. Rather, individuals gradually become dissatisfied over time. This disenchantment often leads to job searches prior to quitting, although not always. The majority of employee turnover research, including hundreds of published studies and popular-press articles, relates to this path by exploring the ways in which employee dissatisfaction leads to intent to leave, the best predictor of leaving, and actual turnover. Certain demographic factors – such as organizational tenure and education level – and attitudinal factors – such as identification with the organization, positive relationships with co-workers and supervisors, and job satisfaction – tend to reduce turnover (C. R. Scott et al., 1999). Those located on the periphery of the organization's communication network also seem to be more likely to be dissatisfied and to exit voluntarily (Feeley, 2004). Although this is the most studied path of voluntary exit, most studies fail to distinguish between this and the other three paths. Failure to consider multiple paths for voluntary exit may explain the lower-than-expected relationships between dissatisfaction and turnover.

Communication for this path likely involves discussion of disenchantment with various friends and relatives. Individuals may attempt to keep their dissatisfaction secret from supervisors for fear of consequences ranging from receiving reduced raises to being fired, but they may discuss it with close co-workers. The individuals probably make formal announcements about quitting either when a new job has been secured or after reaching a decision to quit without a new job. This allows for an exit event, but its scope may be limited. If the dissatisfied employee has created negative peer relationships or been a short-time employee, it may be that only close friends or other dissatisfied employees are involved in an event held away from the workplace.

Other motivations for voluntary exits. Although these four paths provide a fairly comprehensive typology for voluntary turnover, some types of voluntary turnover do not easily fit these classifications or can be the result of various paths. Three of these are discussed briefly.

One motivation for turnover that does not easily fit into the

174

typology occurs when individuals are recruited for other jobs. Top employees are often approached by other companies or hiring firms recruiting for companies. Typically, this recruitment occurs with higher-ranking or highly specialized employees. Although sometimes a disenchanted employee or one who has experienced a shock at work will approach these recruitment firms, individuals approached by these so-called "head hunter" firms often are not looking for another position. Scholars have not generally studied this type of voluntary turnover.

Career changes can lead to voluntary turnover through any of the four paths. Career changes do not involve taking similar jobs in different organizations, but instead changing the type of work, for example from computer analyst to photographer, or from lawyer to social worker. Research suggests that career changes occur for various reasons. Individuals make career changes to pursue life-long dreams, in response to a sense of calling – especially to religious or service occupations – or due to disenchantment with current careers (Tan, 2008). The catalyst for these career changes could be connected to any of the four paths. Some planned exits are specifically related to career changes, such as when someone completes educational or training requirements, but a spouse taking a job in a new community can also be the catalyst for pursuing a new career. Shocks and disenchantment can motivate individuals to pursue alternative careers that had been on hold for some time.

Communication surrounding career changes is often like that of other planned changes in which friends, relatives, and co-workers are involved in communication surrounding the decision to make the career change. However, some individuals wish to keep their desire to change secret. This secrecy seems especially prevalent when individuals move from higher-status positions to lower-status ones, such as from a law firm partner to a restaurant entrepreneur. For example, Tan (2008) found that individuals involved in a downwardly mobile career change sometimes kept the change secret from relatives and close friends until after the transition, and in some cases until long after it had occurred. Regardless of the motivation for the career change and the communication involved while exiting the previous career, those career and organizational experiences become part of the anticipatory socialization of the new career.

Retirement is another form of voluntary turnover that does not fit neatly into one path. Although there are instances where retirement is forced or strongly encouraged and so not completely voluntary, many individuals choose the time of their retirement. As such, retirement is often a planned exit in which individuals know the date weeks, months, or years in advance. However, shocks due to changes at work, such as a new management team or a change in the organization's financial viability, may cause a change in the retirement date.

Research by Avery and Jablin (1988) suggests that, prior to retirement, individuals increase their communication to spouses and family members as they decide to retire and plan for post-retirement. Simultaneously, they tend to decrease communication to work contacts as they reduce work involvement, especially long-term projects. In addition, individuals planning on retiring often increase contacts to nonwork people as they plan post-retirement activities. This may include social, religious, hobby-related, or volunteer groups. In some instances the new contacts concern future employment since many retirees actually continue working, part-time or full-time, in less stressful jobs. Retirees frequently experience ceremonial events at work and elsewhere to mark their retirement, ranging from fairly elaborate, formal affairs with gifts at rented halls to informal activities such as a lunch with friends. These events allow co-workers and friends to celebrate the retiree's voluntary exit.

A number of significant changes occur after retirement (Avery & Jablin, 1988). Retirees quickly feel the loss of peer/work communication networks as they are no longer involved in the daily tasks and have reduced interest in those activities. Communication with spouses and family members becomes much more common, frequently leading to adjustments for all parties involved. Communication to work reduces significantly, with retirement and retirement benefits officers becoming the most frequent contacts, and even those becoming relatively infrequent.

A few individuals hang on to their work roles after retirement. This seems to occur particularly if their self-esteem and identity are highly associated with their work roles. Emeritus professors who continue to maintain regular office hours, conduct research, and work with students perhaps epitomize these individuals. For these people, organizational disengagement is a slow, drawn-out process, perhaps lasting years. For most other individuals, retirement marks the end of organizational membership as employees, unless they start new part-time or full-time jobs. Those who continue to be employees or volunteers bring their years of experience to the new position as part of their anticipatory socialization.

The voluntary exit process

Research on voluntary exit suggests important psychological and communication changes during the process (Jablin, 2001). Wilson (1983) found that individuals involved in voluntary turnover go through a psychological pattern that influences their communication and behaviors. First, during the *pre-announcement phase*, individuals experience unmet expectations at work. These may be related to shocks or gradual disenchantment. In addition, the individuals differentiate themselves from others. For example, they may view themselves as having more opportunities or skills than their co-workers. This differentiation may be an effort at cognitive dissonance reduction to provide additional reasons for leaving. Most likely, they practice reduced job involvement as well. They probably continue meeting their necessary job requirements, but they may volunteer less for extra responsibilities or complete tasks at acceptable, but lower, standards. They may also avoid others as a result of reduced involvement.

The pre-announcement phase is the decision making phase of the process. During this time individuals gather information and communicate with others to determine whether they should disengage from the organization. Depending on the motivation for leaving, this process can be quite open or secretive. For example, in planned exits including retirements, individuals may openly discuss the topic with supervisors, human resource personnel, co-workers, and friends, as they gather information to determine the cost-benefit ratio of continuing. In other instances, such as general disenchantment with the workplace, communication may be much more discriminating. Klatzke (2008) found that individuals were very selective regarding whom they discussed their possible departures with, particularly if they were conducting a job search. They did not want to jeopardize their current positions until they were certain about their futures. Much of the pre-announcement communication was designed to confirm a decision to leave and so communication was often targeted at those they expected to support their decisions.

Although individuals discuss leaving privately during the pre-announcement phase, the *announcement phase* involves the public announcement of the decision. Here the reason for the departure may not be completely forthcoming. In the case of retirements or planned exits, individuals may state their actual reasons for exiting, but in other cases, they may publicly attribute their departures to opportunities or other positive outcomes rather than discuss the shocks or disenchantment that actually led to their decisions. Research by Klatzke (2008) found that individuals created different leave-taking messages for different audiences. Often their message goal was to keep options open and to make sure that they could receive positive references or even be rehired in the future. These findings suggest that exit interviews may have limited value for organizations attempting to discover reasons for turnover.

During this movement toward exit, many individuals develop concern for the system (Wilson, 1983). They may want to help to find and train their replacements. They may leave their jobs in immaculate order or provide detailed instructions on work procedures they used. Due to their prior commitment to their workplace and co-workers, they attempt to leave the workplace in good order to prevent problems after they depart and to make sure they are not blamed for any problems that do occur.

The *exit phase* begins once individuals officially become former employees. Like in retirement, communication with former employees quickly becomes limited and often challenging. Although individuals may meet with former co-workers, work discussions quickly become problematic, because either the former employees no longer have the knowledge or interest to participate in the conversation or current employees are unable to openly discuss topics due to confidentiality issues (Klatzke, 2008). As a result, communication focuses on nonwork topics. If nonwork topics were never the basis for the relationships, they may not maintain the relationships after exit. In addition, former employees have new communication contacts, and time issues make it more difficult to continue to interact. As a result, communication typically becomes infrequent.

The workgroup also is actively involved in sense-making during the exit process. If during the pre-announcement phase, the individual's gradual withdrawal is apparent, the workgroup may begin discussing explanations or rumors about potential exits. After the official announcement, the workgroup makes sense of the departure. They may agree upon explanations that only partially take into account the explanations given by the departing employee, particularly if they have common scripts for departing employees.

Wilson (1983) and Jablin (2001) provide a useful framework for studying voluntary exit, but, like other researchers, fail to recognize the various paths identified above. The presence and duration of these phases likely differs according to the path. For example, while all three phases would be of significant length in a planned exit, a shock leading to quitting immediately would potentially eliminate any pre-announcement phase and lead to the announcement and exit phases being essentially combined. Concern for the system is probably more common in planned exits than in gradual disenchantments.

Involuntary exit

Certain forms of involuntary exit have been discussed in a previous chapter. For example, reductions-in-force result in involuntary exit for some employees. Mergers and acquisitions can result in involuntary exit when departments are consolidated or eliminated. Instead of involuntary exits resulting from organizational changes, the focus here is on specific individuals being targeted for involuntary exit. Various terms are used to describe the process of employees having to leave an organization against their will. Some of the more common terms include being fired, dismissed, terminated, or let go.

In many organizations, certain behaviors result in immediate dismissals. For example, illegal activities such as stealing, drug or alcohol abuse, or blatant sexual harassment, as well as gross insubordination, frequently result in individuals being fired on the spot, or what are sometimes called "summary dismissals". Other actions, such as excessive lateness or absence, may similarly result in immediate dismissals if they occur during employees' probationary periods. The actions that result in summary dismissals should be specified in a work agreement or contract, but in reality many employees are "hired-at-will" and are not covered by specific agreements (Granholm, 1991).

Many involuntary exits result from the employer's gradual disenchantment with the employee's performance over time. For these employees, the dismissal process is often described as "progressive discipline." Progressive discipline differs from summary dismissals in that a series of steps are taken to hopefully retain the employee, and dismissal occurs only when those steps fail. Progressive discipline centers around three communication activities: a problem-solving breakpoint, an elimination breakpoint, and a dismissal meeting (Cox & Kramer, 1995; Fairhurst, Green, & Snavely, 1984).

Problem-solving breakpoint

Supervisors/employers often deal with less-than-ideal workers. Instead of taking action with these employees, supervisors often hope these employees will improve over time with the help of informal suggestions from peers and supervisors. Supervisors are often reluctant to take more specific actions because they have a general dislike for dismissing employees, have an optimistic belief that – given time and additional chances – things will improve, or hired the employee initially and have invested too much in training to admit to a problem. Despite these hindrances to acting, at some point the evidence becomes overwhelming, from either co-workers' or customers' complaints or productivity records, and the problem-solving breakpoint is reached (Fairhurst et al., 1984). At this point, the supervisor believes that additional formal training and education is needed to improve the employee's performance.

At the problem-solving breakpoint, the supervisor–subordinate relationship changes from one of working together to one of controlling the problem employee. The supervisor uses more formal communication to explicitly address performance problems. This involves making expectations clearer and providing training to improve performance. The supervisor may explicitly define tardiness and the number of tardies allowed in a given time period, or may provide training for improving customer interactions. At this point, the supervisor attributes the problem to something contextual such as inadequate training and inadequate supervision rather than an employee trait. In addition, the supervisor sees the cost-benefit ratio of retaining the employee through training and education as better than the cost-benefit ratio of dismissing the employee and hiring a replacement. When this more formal interaction at the problem-solving breakpoint results in improvements, there is no need for further action. However, popular advice books recommend documenting the problems and corrective activities at this point so that, if improvements do not occur, it is easier to dismiss the employee at a later date (Granholm, 1991).

Elimination breakpoint

When the efforts surrounding the problem-solving breakpoint fail to create acceptable employee performance, the elimination breakpoint is reached (Fairhurst et al., 1984). Here, the supervisor changes the attribution for the problem. Instead of attributing the problem to the context, the supervisor identifies the problem as inherent to the employee. Since the problem is an employee trait, not situational, the solution is dismissing the employee. The cost-benefit ratio of retaining the employee is evaluated as significantly worse than the cost-benefit ratio of hiring a replacement. The relationship changes from one of controlling the problem employee to one of eliminating him/her. Documentation continues until there is a preponderance of evidence to support dismissing the employee. Depending on the employment situation, the amount of evidence needed varies significantly. Once the evidence is sufficient, the termination meeting is conducted.

Termination meeting

Popular books on termination meetings provide advice like holding the meeting in a private location, having a witness present, having documentation present, being calm and professional, among other suggestions (Granholm, 1991). Advice varies on issues like when during the week or day to dismiss the employees and other factors to consider. Based on retail employers' actual practices, Cox and Kramer (1995) identified a series of steps that typically occur in termination meetings. The first part of the meeting includes asking the employee about his/her performance and presenting the evidence of the problem and allowing the employee to respond. Employees typically either resign during this part of the meeting or attempt to defend their behaviors. The second half of the meeting includes directly communicating that the employee is being dismissed, after which the employee asks procedural questions about final paychecks or severance packages if any, and the supervisor often offers advice which might include suggestions for employment or ways of improving future performance. If the documentation process has been ongoing, the employee should not be surprised, but emotions can still run high in these meetings. This emotional component is one of the reasons supervisors are reluctant to dismiss employees in the first place.

Sense-making during involuntary exit

Sense-making is important throughout the dismissal process on several levels. At the problem-solving and elimination breakpoints, supervisors retrospectively make sense of the employee's performance. Throughout the interactions with the supervisor, the employee makes sense of his/her performance inadequacies which may involve attributing the problem to the organization or peers or an admission of personal problems. At the termination meeting, at least some level of mutual sense-making occurs as both parties understand that employment has ended.

Sense-making involves more than just the dismissed employee and the supervisor. Prior to dismissal, co-workers must make sense of the continued employment of an underachieving employee. Understanding that peers may conclude that performance quality is unimportant should motivate supervisors to more quickly dismiss poor employees. Co-workers must also make sense after the dismissal occurs. When it is perceived as just, sense-making is probably quite simple and immediate. However, employees who were friends of the dismissed employee or whose performance levels are similar may question their own organizational futures. Because supervisors recognize that news or gossip about dismissals spreads throughout the workforce quickly, in some instances they take steps to inform employees to assist them in sense-making (Cox & Kramer, 1995). So, although dismissing an employee ends their organizational assimilation process, it is part of the ongoing change and adjustment for continuing members.

An alternative exit process

So far, it has been assumed that the distinction between voluntary and involuntary exit is always clear. In a study of employee dismissals, Cox and Kramer (1995) found that the distinction is sometimes ambiguous. They found that supervisors sometimes communicated and behaved in ways that encouraged or induced turnover. A follow-up study by Cox (1999) went further to identify strategies that co-workers used to encourage someone to leave. Some of the strategies used by supervisors were simply the initial steps in the involuntary dismissal process, such as documenting problems or warning workers that their continued employment was in question. Employees would sometimes voluntarily quit early in the process so that the supervisor never actually dismissed them. Other strategies were more indirect and could appear to be empathetic or even supportive of employees. Supervisors and peers reported that they sometimes asked employees if they were happy with their jobs and suggested that they might be more satisfied working in a different career or organization.

Other strategies seemed designed to reduce the cost-benefit ratio of continuing to work so that an individual would quit. For example, a supervisor might schedule the individual for fewer hours or less desirable shifts. Peers might consistently divide tasks so that the individual always receives the least desirable duties. Isolating the individual from communication with peers and supervisors also makes it unpleasant or even difficult to do a job. In perhaps the most negative approach, peers might even sabotage the individual's work resulting in more work or negative evaluations.

Sometimes called "constructive termination," this process of encouraging or inducing turnover can save supervisors from the lengthy process of dismissing employees and save the organization from paying unemployment benefits. This process can also result in lawsuits, even if those accused deny it, if employees believe that their supervisors were aware of what was happening but did nothing or even participated in creating the negative work environment (Rosner, Halcrow, & Levins, 2003). Alternatively, when individuals quit under these circumstances, they may report or feel that they exited voluntarily as the result of a gradual disenchantment with the workplace or may report they quit to find a better job and more supportive co-workers. Individuals who are not part of the organization's majority demographic or culture, who never felt that they became assimilated and who felt that they remained on the organization's fringe, may not be aware that they have been targeted for constructive termination. As a result, it is impossible to know the prevalence of this type of exit due to the difficulty of accurately identifying it. Thus, encouraged or induced exit is likely a common form of organizational exit, but one which is not necessarily accurately reported.

Exit from voluntary associations

The distinction between voluntary and involuntary exit seems somewhat artificial for volunteers. Similar to summary dismissals, there are probably some behaviors which will cause an individual to be asked not to return. For example, an individual who is disruptive to a religious service or who causes other volunteers to quit may be asked to leave. It is unlikely that supervisors would go through the steps of progressive discipline with underperforming volunteers. They are more likely to find some alternative job for them to complete or simply fail to make them aware of volunteer opportunities.

The exit process for most volunteers likely is the result of one of the four paths of voluntary exit. Other life events, which can include work, family, or other life enrichment activities, frequently lead to time-based stress (Greenhaus & Beutell, 1985). Since it is typically easiest to disengage from the voluntary association, it is frequently the first to be eliminated. Volunteers may be motivated to quit by shocks that may be similar to those experienced by employees. Shocks might include not being selected for, or elected to, a certain position or finding that the organization wastes money and time by failing to manage its resources. Gradual disenchantment is also a common reason for volunteers quitting; they find that the organization no longer meets their needs and so they look elsewhere.

One aspect of exit that differs for volunteers is the fluidity of membership. Because entrance and exit requirements are much less formal and structured, volunteers can join and leave repeatedly in most volunteer organizations. This pattern may limit their opportunities for volunteer leadership roles because they are viewed as unreliable compared to steady members, but they are still likely to be accepted. A study of a community choir found that it was common for members to drop out for short periods of time due to various time conflicts, after which they were typically welcomed back; other members seemed to accept this as a natural outcome of volunteer membership since people have other commitments (Kramer, forthcoming).

Conclusion

In the scenario, Avery dealt with three different types of exits. Mackenzie's exit illustrated a planned, voluntary exit related to a nonwork event, graduation from college. Because it was planned, co-workers even threw Mackenzie a farewell party. Payton's exit illustrated the gradual disenchantment process of voluntary exit that has been the focus of most research. What may not have been noticed is that Payton may have experienced some shock at work that led to a job search and exit, or may have been encouraged by peers to leave. Avery may be unaware of Payton's real motivation for exit. Finally, Avery has been involved in progressive discipline in dismissing Corey from work. Only the last step remained, the dismissal meeting.

Organizational exit is an inevitable conclusion of the assimilation process as individuals leave all the organizations that they join at some point. The process of leaving includes voluntary and involuntary exits, although the distinction is not always clear. The process of exit is steeped in social exchange evaluations as individuals consider whether the cost-benefit ratio justifies maintaining organizational memberships. It also involves sense-making as the individuals leaving make sense of their departure and those remaining make sense of the consequences of that departure for themselves.

9

———

Epilogue

The preceding chapters have presented a generally positive view of socialization/assimilation processes although certainly some negative aspects have been presented. Sometimes individuals fail to adjust to their organizational roles, never fitting in, or, after becoming established members, they become dissatisfied over time and leave. Sometimes organizational decision makers decide that they must downsize or terminate employees. But overall, the picture of socialization processes and the supporting research seems generally positive. Rather than leaving this fairly rosy picture unscathed, this chapter considers two areas of concern with the socialization research presented so far: a dark side of socialization and criticism or issues related to the research.

A dark side of socialization

An assumption so far has been that the socialization processes and outcomes are appropriate. The few negative outcomes that occur are generally associated with those who do not success-fully complete the socialization process and exit as a result. It is assumed that those who become members generally benefit from their organizational membership. Although most organizations do not resemble *Star Trek*'s The Borg in which people experi-ence a complete loss of identity and free will, at times successful socialization has extremely negative effects on members. Some of these negative outcomes occur at a societal level, such as in cases of genocide against a particular group, like the Jews at the hands of the Nazis during World War II. In other instances, the negative outcomes occur at a group or organizational level, such as when the members of the People's Temple committed mass suicide at the direction of their leader Reverend Jim Jones in 1978.

A study by Cushman (1986) explores the communication and psychological processes that lead to this dark side of socialization using slightly less dire examples: the Unification Church and Scientology. Cushman describes factors that contribute to the indoctrination processes of these restrictive groups. First, the individuals recruited for these groups or cults tend to have experienced a significant rejection by family, work, or society. This makes them vulnerable with strong needs for affiliation. The groups fill this need by offering acceptance under very restricted conditions.

According to Cushman (1986), among the important strategies these groups use to socialize the recruits is milieu control, in which the recruits are not allowed to communicate with outsiders who might offer resistive messages. In addition, the groups create a mystical aura around their belief system and leaders. Deification of the leader and positioning group doctrines over individuals creates a system in which questioning anything is inappropriate. These groups demand that recruits accept their beliefs completely or they will withhold the affiliation recruits so desperately desire. By attacking the recruits' cultural frame of reference so totally and then reinforcing the new beliefs by having them recruit others, the indoctrination or socialization is completed. Given this process of indoctrination, it is not surprising that it often takes deprogramming interventions to de-socialize former cult members.

It is unlikely that anyone would accuse major corporations of practicing this sort of indoctrination in their socialization processes. Few could obtain this level of compliance even if they desired it. Yet the differences between the practices of cults and those of other organizations often seem to be ones of degree. Union motor workers in Detroit are unlikely to drive foreign-made cars. Professors are unlikely to question the value of a college education or their right to tenure. Food bank volunteers probably do not question whether the program helps to alleviate or perpetuate poverty. Although examples like these are nothing close to milieu control, they indicate that attitudes and behaviors can become narrowly confined through socialization.

In considering this dark side of socialization, it seems that a number of characteristics make it unique. Perhaps the most important difference appears to be the almost complete lack of personalization in these situations and the corresponding dominance of socialization. The rather complete control of appearance, activities, and thoughts precludes any resistance or personalization. Another important difference is that these extreme forms control individuals 24 hours a day, not just during the work day. So, although extreme forms of socialization are probably not major concerns in most settings, considering them creates a wariness of socialization.

Issues and criticisms

It would be unusual if a well-established research line in the social sciences was not criticized by some scholars. Socialization research is no exception. A public discussion of some concerns was presented in the December 1999 issue of *Communication Monographs*. Rather than summarizing or rehashing those discussions, a few major issues or controversies will be considered here.

General versus individual experiences

In setting out to develop the study of socialization, Van Maanen and Schein (1979) stated that one of their main assumptions is that they should not become: "too preoccupied with individual characteristics (age, background, personality characteristics, etc.), specific organizations (public, private, voluntary, coercive, etc.), or particular occupations (doctor, lawyer, crook, banker, etc.). To be of value to researchers and laymen alike, the theory must transcend the particular and peculiar and aim for the general and typical" (p. 216). Much of the research and most of this book have maintained this focus on developing a general understanding of socialization.

This focus on a general understanding of socialization creates a number of issues. The most prominent issue is that it seems to devalue individual experiences, and in particular the unique experiences of people who are not part of the dominant demographics or attitudes of organizations. Those individuals have experiences that differ from the sort of general trajectories that the research projects (Bullis & Stout, 2000). For example, women are often in the minority in certain occupations and may have socialization experiences that differ significantly from men's. Dallimore (2003) documented some of the ways in which the experiences new women faculty members were different from men's, including having fewer role models, managing more work–family issues, having to work harder to build credibility with students and peers, and a lack of informal network opportunities. Allen (1996) discusses how her experiences as a woman of color in the academy were different from those of other men and women. Similarly, the socialization experiences of men in predominantly female occupations such as nursing are different from those for women. Members of other groups, whether they are defined by factors like race, religion, socio-economic status, political affiliation, sexual identity, ability, or age, also have experiences that are unique (Allen, 2004). As a result, there continues to be an issue of whether to focus socialization research on factors related to individual experiences or more general conceptual and theoretical issues.

A related issue is the negative effect that focusing on general experiences can have on individuals. Treating the general experiences of the dominant group as the normative socialization experience implies that those with different experiences are not normative. This process has been described as constructing the non-dominant experience as the "other" (Dallimore, 2003). The othering process implicitly marginalizes those who do not share the general or dominant experience, which then makes inclusion or full membership problematic. Organizational members from under-represented groups may never feel fully accepted because their socialization experiences are considered different and may feel that they are outsiders within the organization (Bullis & Stout, 2000). Since even individuals who are members of the dominant demographic or attitudinal group may have individual experiences that differ from the general experience, they may also feel marginalized to some degree. For example, a white male professor at a small liberal arts college who values research more than his peers may experience dissonance during the socialization process that leads him to feel that he will always be on the organization's fringe. By focusing on describing general socialization experiences, the research on and practical application of socialization concepts creates psychological barriers for those who feel that their experiences are different from the norm.

Since these are largely level-of-analysis issues, it is important to recognize the value of examining socialization from multiple levels. There is value both in examining individual experiences and in developing models and understandings at the general or organizational level.

Domination, resistance, and individualization

When socialization efforts maintain the status quo, they produce and reproduce relationships of domination and subordination that marginalize certain individuals (Bullis & Stout, 2000). This happens quite clearly in settings like military training, but the extent to which this occurs in other settings is unclear since there is evidence that individuals do not conform particularly well to socialization efforts (Kramer & Miller, 1999). What is needed is a more thorough examination of how organizational members enact resistance when they do not accept these organizational socialization efforts and attempt to change the status quo (Bullis, 1993), and how individuals personalize or change the organization to meet their needs (Kramer & Miller, 1999). A more thorough examination of resistance and personalization will provide a deeper understanding of how organizations are reproduced and changed through the socialization process. Similarly, more research should explore how individuals understand and respond to organizational socialization efforts since individuals do not respond uniformly to this process. They may heartily agree with some messages, cope, accommodate, or comply with others, stubbornly resist some, and actively work to change others. Refusing offers or exiting represent forms of resistance in some cases. Understanding these varied responses by individuals, and across individuals and groups, will provide a better understanding of the socialization process.

Use of phase models

A major criticism of the socialization research is that it relies on models that inappropriately present the process as a linear progression. One of the problems with stage or phase models and theories is that they "are hard to live with and hard to live without" (Planalp, 2003, p. 90). The drawings of these models provide a useful picture to assist in understanding the concepts, but are limited in their ability to capture the phenomenon's complexity. The drawings appear quite linear, even when they include multiple boxes and multi-directional arrows. Despite this appearance, most researchers recognize this problem and emphasize in their texts that the process is much more fluid. For example, Feldman (1981) wrote that there is overlap and continuity between stages. Jones (1986) emphasized that socialization does not always occur the same way in terms of order, duration, and content. Jablin (2001) pointed out that none of the communication activities, processes, or outcomes were distinctly associated with any particular part of the assimilation process and were ongoing throughout it. Given these sorts of clarifications, it seems that the criticism of the research for being too linear oversimplifies what is universally recognized as non-linear and complex. The socialization models are a convenient metaphor or visual representation that assist in understanding; like all models and metaphors, they cannot capture the entire process. Alternative conceptualizations should be considered for what they add to the understanding of the process without dismissing current models.

Container metaphor

Another criticism is that the socialization literature is restricted by its reliance on the organization-as-container metaphor suggested by language such as joining and leaving, or going into and out of the organization (Bullis, 1993; R. C. Smith & Turner, 1995). Researchers use this language because most naïve participants use that same language to describe their experiences (Kramer & Miller, 1999). When organizational members use language like insider and outsider, member and nonmember, it becomes difficult to represent their lived experiences without using language that suggests a container metaphor. Even terms like "outsider within" rely on boundary language to present alternative perspectives (Bullis & Stout, 2000). As a result, it becomes important to discuss ways in which the container metaphor both enables and constrains researchers, rather than attempting to eliminate it. In addition, most organizational scholars, including socialization researchers, agree with a bona fide group perspective (Putnam & Stohl, 1996) which recognizes that organizational boundaries are permeable and difficult to define. The language of boundaries and containers is beneficial for describing many people's experiences, but should not be presented as a rigid, inflexible view of organizations.

Broader socialization concerns

Clair (1996) criticizes organizational socialization models for devaluing certain types of work, such as the self-employed and artists, for example. She clearly states she is interested in broader issues than socializing individuals into organizations, such as the meaning of labor or how social order is established and maintained (Clair, 1999). There certainly is much to be learned about socialization as part of participation in society in various capacities, not just for paid employment, but it simply represents a different focus. A focus on organizational socialization does not devalue broader societal socialization issues any more than focusing on volunteering devalues paid employment. The current volume attempts to broaden the focus of organizational socialization by including volunteer membership, something Jablin (2001) explicitly excluded. The study of various forms of organizational membership increases the understanding of organizational socialization. The study of various types of work increases the understanding of work socialization at the societal level.

Continuing concerns

Other concerns continue to be problematic. For example, indicative of a management bias, there continues to be far more focus on how organizations influence individuals rather than on how individuals influence organizations through resistance or personalization. This type of management bias is unlikely to end soon.

There is much more focus on how individuals experience transitions (e.g. newcomer, retiree) than on how the surrounding workgroup experiences these changes. For example, we know far more about newcomer experiences than we do about the experiences of co-workers who must interact with newcomers as part of their ongoing socialization. This volume attempts to include a more systemic view of these changes in some places, but there is more work to be done.

With few exceptions, the focus continues to be on socialization of paid employees without consideration of socialization processes involved in other forms of organizational membership. The brief discussions of volunteers in this volume are only a starting point for changing this. There are many different types of voluntary memberships, from people who write occasional checks to support a cause to individuals involved in leadership roles. The range of membership experiences should be explored more thoroughly.

Conclusion

This volume provides a general understanding of the socialization process, from prior to entering organizations to exiting them. There certainly are significant amounts of additional scholarly literature that could be included. No doubt it would be possible to double the number of references. Those included are simply representative of the types of research conducted. Similarly, this brief epilogue touches on only a few issues to be addressed in future research. This is not meant to be a comprehensive list of issues, just a starting point. The fact that there is more to be done does not indicate that what has been done is insignificant, just incomplete.

Organizational socialization is a common experience in society today. Like most people, I can name dozens of organizations that I have participated in at some level in the last few years, not to mention in my lifetime. Hopefully, readers of this book have increased their understanding of the socialization process in ways that will benefit them. For a few, it may help them develop a scholarly understanding of this topic so that they can research new areas of socialization. For others, it may help them to make sense of, and reduce uncertainty about, their own organizational experiences. By increasing our understanding of organizational socialization, we develop a better understanding of our organizational experiences.

References

Adkins, C. L., Russell, C. J. & Werbel, J. D. (1994). Judgments of fit in the selection process: the role of work value congruence. *Personnel Psychology*, 47, 605–23.

Allen, B. J. (1996). Feminist standpoint theory: a black woman's (re)view of organizational socialization. *Communication Studies*, 43, 257–71.

Allen, B. J. (2000). "Learning the ropes": a black feminist standpoint analysis. In P. M. Buzzanell (ed.), *Rethinking organizational & managerial communication from feminist perspectives* (pp. 177–208). Thousand Oaks, CA: Sage.

Allen, B. J. (2004). *Difference matters*. Long Grove, IL: Waveland Press.

Altman, I. & Taylor, D. (1973). *Social penetration: the development of interpersonal relationships*. New York: Holt.

Alvesson, M., Ashcraft, K. L. & Thomas, R. (2008). Identity matters: reflections on the construction of identity scholarship in organization studies. *Organization*, 15, 5–28.

Andrews, P. (2000). Part a. Inside Microsoft. In G. L. Peterson (ed.), *Communicating in organizations: a casebook* (pp. 17–24). Boston: Allyn and Bacon.

Ashford, S. J. & Black, J. S. (1996). Proactivity during organizational entry: the role of desire for control. *Journal of Applied Psychology*, 81, 99–124.

Ashforth, B. E., Kreiner, G. E. & Fugate, M. (2000). All in a day's work: boundaries and micro role transitions. *Academy of Management Review*, 25, 472–91.

Ashforth, B. E. & Mael, F. A. (1989). Social identity theory and the organization. *Academy of Management Review*, 14, 20–39.

Ashforth, B. E. & Saks, A. M. (1996). Socialization tactics: longitudinal effects on newcomer adjustment. *Academy of Management Journal*, 39, 149–78.

Avery, C. M. & Jablin, F. M. (1988). Retirement preparation programs and organizational communication. *Communication Education*, 37, 68–80.

References

Bain, P. & Taylor, P. (2000). Entrapped by the "electronic panopticon?" Worker resistance in the call centre. *New Technology, Work and Employment*, 15, 1–18.

Ballinger, G. A. & Schoorman, F. D. (2007). Individual reaction to leadership succession in workgroups. *Academy of Management Review*, 32, 118–36.

Balogun, J. & Johnson, G. (2004). Organizational restructuring and middle manager sensemaking. *Academy of Management Journal*, 47, 523–49.

Barge, J. K. & Schlueter, D. W. (2004). Memorable messages and newcomer socialization. *Western Journal of Communication*, 68, 233–56.

Barker, J. R. (1993). Tightening the iron cage: concertive control in self-managing teams. *Administrative Science Quarterly*, 38, 408–37.

Bastien, D. T. (1992). Change in organizational culture: the use of linguistic methods in a corporate acquisition. *Management Communication Quarterly*, 5, 403–42.

Berger, C. R. (1979). Beyond initial interactions: uncertainty, understanding, and the development of interpersonal relationships. In H. Giles & R. N. St. Clair (eds.), *Language and social psychology* (pp. 122–44). Baltimore: University Park Press.

Berger, C. R. & Bradac, J. J. (1982). *Language and social knowledge: uncertainty in interpersonal relations*. London: Edward Arnold.

Berger, C. R. & Calabrese, R. J. (1975). Some explorations in initial interaction and beyond: toward a developmental theory of interpersonal communication. *Human Communication Research*, 1, 99–112.

Bluedorn, A. C. (1978). A taxonomy of turnover. *Academy of Management Review*, 3, 647–51.

Boezeman, E. J. & Ellemers, N. (2008). Volunteer recruitment: the role of organizational support and anticipated respect in non-volunteers' attraction to charitable volunteer organizations. *Journal of Applied Psychology*, 93, 1013–26.

Brashers, D. E. (2001). Communication and uncertainty management. *Journal of Communication*, 51, 477–97.

Brashers, D. E., Goldsmith, D. J. & Hsieh, E. (2002). Information seeking and avoiding in health contexts. *Human Communication Research*, 28, 258–71.

Breaugh, J. A. & Starke, M. (2000). Research on employee recruitment: so many studies, so many remaining questions. *Journal of Management*, 26, 405–34.

Brett, J. M. (1982). Job transfer and well being. *Journal of Applied Psychology*, 67, 450–63.

Brett, J. M. & Werbel, J. D. (1980). *The effect of job transfer on employees and their families*. Washington, DC: Employee Relocation Council.

Brochner, J., Grover, S., O'Malley, M. N., Reed, T. F. & Glynn, M. A. (1993). Threat of future layoffs, self-esteem, and survivors' reactions: evidence from the laboratory and the field. *Strategic Management Journal*, 14, 153–66.

Brown, M. H. (1985). That reminds me of a story: speech action in organizational socialization. *Western Journal of Speech Communication*, 49, 27–42.

References

Bullis, C. (1993). Organizational socialization research: enabling, constraining, and shifting perspectives. *Communication Monographs*, 60, 10–17.

Bullis, C. & Stout, K. R. (2000). Organizational socialization: a feminist standpoint approach. In P. M. Buzzanell (ed.), *Rethinking organizational and managerial communication from feminist perspectives* (pp. 47–75). Thousand Oaks, CA: Sage.

Bureau of Labor Statistics (2009). *Volunteering in the United States, 2008.* Washington, DC: US Government Printing Office. Available at www.bls.gov/news.release/volun.nr0.htm. Accessed August 12, 2009.

Cantor, N., Mischel, W. & Schwartz, J. (1982). Social knowledge: structure, content, use and abuse. In A. H. Hastrof & A. M. Isen (eds.), *Cognitive social psychology* (pp. 33–72). New York: Elsevier-North Holland.

Carlone, D. (2001). Enablement, constraint, and *The 7 habits of highly effective people. Management Communication Quarterly*, 14, 491–7.

Carver, C. S. & Scheier, M. F. (1990). Origins and functions of positive and negative affect: a control-process view. *Psychological Review*, 19–35.

Casey, M. K., Miller, V. D. & Johnson, J. R. (1997). Survivors' information seeking following a reduction in workforce. *Communication Research*, 24, 755–81.

Center for American Women and Politics. (2009). *Fact sheet: women in elective office 2009.* New Brunswick, NJ: Rutgers. Available at www.cawp.rutgers.edu/fast_facts/levels_of_office/documents/elective.pdf. Accessed February 6, 2009.

Chansler, P. A., Swamidass, P. M. & Cortlandt, C. (2003). Self-managing work teams: an empirical study of group cohesiveness in "natural work groups" at a Harley-Davidson Motor Company plant. *Small Group Research*, 34, 101–20.

Chao, G. T., O'Leary-Kelly, A. M., Wolf, S., Klein, H. J. & Garner, P. D. (1994). Organizational socialization: its content and consequences. *Journal of Applied Psychology*, 79, 730–43.

Chao, G. T., Walz, P. M. & Gardner, P. D. (1992). Formal and informal mentorships: a comparison on mentoring functions and contrast with nonmentored counterparts. *Personnel Psychology*, 45, 619–36.

Cheney, G. (1991). *Rhetoric in an organizational society: managing multiple identities.* Columbia, SC: University of South Carolina Press.

Clair, R. P. (1996). The political nature of the colloquialism, "a real job": implications for organizational socialization. *Communication Monographs*, 63, 249–67.

Clair, R. P. (1999). Ways of seeing: a review of Kramer and Miller's manuscript. *Communication Monographs*, 66, 374–81.

Clapham, S. E. & Schwenk, C. R. (1991). Self-serving attributions, managerial cognition, and company performance. *Strategic Management Journal*, 12, 219–29.

Collins, C. J. (2007). The interactive effects of recruitment practices and product awareness on job seekers' employer knowledge and application behaviors. *Journal of Applied Psychology*, 92, 180–90.

Cornett-DeVito, M. M. & Friedman, P. G. (1995). Communication processes and merger success: an exploratory study of four financial institution mergers. *Management Communication Quarterly*, 9, 46–77.

Corporation for National and Community Service (2007). *Issue brief: volunteer retention*. Washington, DC: author. Available at http://agweb.okstate.edu/fourh/focus/2007/may/attachments/VIA_brief_retention.pdf. Accessed June 5, 2009.

Cotter, D. A., Hermsen, J. M. & Vanneman, R. (2004). *The American people: gender inequality at work*. New York: Russell Page Foundation.

Cox, S. A. (1999). Group communication and employee turnover: how coworkers encourage voluntary turnover. *Southern Journal of Communication*, 64, 181–92.

Cox, S. A. & Kramer, M. W. (1995). Communication during employee dismissals: social exchange principles and group influences on employee exit. *Management Communication Quarterly*, 9, 156–90.

Cushman, P. (1986). The self besieged: recruitment–indoctrination processes in restrictive groups. *Journal of the Theory of Social Behavior*, 16, 1–32.

Dallimore, E. J. (2003). Memorable messages as discursive formations: the gendered socialization of new university faculty. *Women's Studies in Communication*, 26, 214–65.

Daniel, T. A. & Metcalf, G. S. (2001). *The management of people in mergers and acquisitions*. Westport, CT: Quorum Books.

Deal, T. E. (1985). Cultural change: opportunity, silent killer, or metamorphosis? In R. Kilmann, M. Saxton, & R. Serpa (eds.), *Gaining control of the corporate culture* (pp. 292–331). San Francisco: Jossey-Bass.

Dewey, J. (1910). *How we think*. Boston, MA: D. C. Heath & Co.

DiFonzo, N. & Bordia, P. (1998). A tale of two corporations: managing uncertainty during organizational change. *Human Resource Management*, 37, 295–303.

DiSanza, J. R. (1995). Bank teller organizational assimilation in a system of contradictory practices. *Management Communication Quarterly*, 9, 191–218.

Dougherty, D. S. & Krone, K. J. (2000). Overcoming the dichotomy: cultivating standpoints in organizations through research. *Women's Studies in Communication*, 23, 16–40.

Dougherty, D. S. & Smythe, M. J. (2004). Sensemaking, organizational culture, and sexual harassment. *Journal of Applied Communication Research*, 32, 293–317.

Drago, R. W. (2007). *Striking a balance: work, family, life*. Boston, MA: Economic Affairs Bureau.

Eisenberg, E. M., Monge, P. R. & Miller, K. I. (1983). Involvement in communication networks as a predictor of organizational commitment. *Human Communication Research*, 10, 179–201.

Elsbach, K. D., Sutton, R. I. & Principe, K. E. (1998). Averting expected challenges through anticipatory impression management: a study of hospital billing. *Organizational Science*, 9, 68–86.

England, G. W. & Whitely, W. T. (1990) Cross-national meanings of working. In A. P. Brief and W. R. Nord (eds), *Meanings of occupational work: a collection of essays* (pp. 65–106). Lexington, MA: Lexington Books.

Engler-Parish, P. G. & Millar, F. E. (1989). An exploratory relational control analysis of the employment screening interview. *Western Journal of Speech Communication*, 53, 30–51.

Ensher, E. A. & Murphy, S. E. (1997). Effects of race, gender, perceived similarity, and contact on mentor relationships. *Journal of Vocational Behavior*, 50, 460–81.

Fagenson, E. A. (1989). The mentor advantage: perceived career/job experiences of protégés versus non-protégés. *Journal of Organizational Behavior*, 10, 309–20.

Fairhurst, G. T. & Chandler, T. A. (1989). Social structures in leader–member interaction. *Communication Monographs*, 56, 215–39.

Fairhurst, G. T., Green, S. G. & Snavely, B. K. (1984). Managerial control and discipline: whips and chains. In R. N. Bostrom & B. H. Westley (eds.), *Communication yearbook 8* (pp. 558–93). Beverly Hills, CA: Sage.

Falbe, C. M. & Yukl, G. (1992). Consequences for managers of using single influence tactics and combinations of tactics. *Academy of Management Journal*, 35, 638–52.

Fayol, H. (1949). *General and industrial management*. Translated from the French edn. (Dunod) by Constance Storrs. London: Pitman.

Feeley, T. H. (1999). Testing a communication network model of employee turnover based on centrality. *Journal of Applied Communication Research*, 28, 262–77.

Feldman, D. C. (1976). A contingency theory of socialization. *Administrative Science Quarterly*, 21, 433–52.

Feldman, D. C. (1981). The multiple socialization of organization members. *Academy of Management Review*, 6, 209–318.

Feldman, D. C. & Brett, J. M. (1983). Coping with new jobs: a comparative study of new hires and job changers. *Academy of Management Journal*, 26, 258–72.

Feldman, D. C. & Weitz, B. A. (1990). Summer interns: factors contributing to positive development experiences. *Journal of Vocational Behavior*, 37, 267–84.

Finkelstein, L. M., Kulas, J. T. & Dages, K. D. (2003). Age differences in proactive newcomer socialization strategies in two populations. *Journal of Business and Psychology*, 17, 473–502.

Fisher, R. J. & Ackerman, D. (1998). The effects of recognition and group need on volunteerism: a social norm perspective. *Journal of Consumer Research*, 25, 262–75.

Foa, U. G. & Foa, E. B. (1980). Resource theory: interpersonal behavior as exchange. In K. J. Gergen, M. S. Greenberg, & R. H. Willis (eds.), *Social exchange: advances in theory and research* (pp. 77–94). New York: Plenum.

Forward, G. L. & Scheerhornd, D. (1996). Identities and the assimilation process in the modern organization. In H. B. Mokros (ed.), *Interaction & identity*, (Vol. V, pp. 371–91). New Brunswick, NJ: Transaction Publishing.

Foucault, M. (1984). Panopticism (Discipline and punish: the birth of the prison). In P. Rabinow (ed.), *Foucault reader* (pp. 206–13). New York: Pantheon Books.

Fritz, J. M. H. (1997). Responses to unpleasant work relationships. *Communication Research Reports*, 14, 302–11.

Fritz, J. M. H. (2006). Typology of troublesome others at work: a follow-up study. In J. M. H. Fritz and B. L. Omdahl (eds.), *Communicating in the workplace with difficult others* (pp. 21–46). New York: Peter Lang.

Frone, M. R., Russell, M. & Cooper, M. L. (1992). Antecedents and outcomes of work–family conflict: testing a model of the work–family interface. *Journal of Applied Psychology*, 77, 65–78.

Gallagher, E. B. & Sias, P. M. (2009). The new employee as a source of uncertainty: veteran employee information seeking about new hires. *Western Journal of Communication*, 73, 23–46.

Gibson, M. K. & Papa, M. J. (2000). The mud, the blood, and the beer guys: organizational osmosis in blue-collar work groups. *Journal of Applied Communication Research*, 28, 68–88.

Gioia, D. A. & Chittipeddi, K. (1991). Sensemaking and sensegiving in strategic change initiation. *Strategic Management Journal*, 12, 433–48.

Glick, P., Wilk, K. & Perreault, M. (1995). Images of occupations: components of gender and status in occupational stereotypes. *Sex Roles*, 32, 565–82.

Goodnow, J. J. (1988). Children's household work: its nature and functions. *Psychological Bulletin*, 103, 5–26.

Graen, G. B. (2003). Interpersonal workplace theory at the crossroads. In G. B. Graen (ed.), *Dealing with diversity: LMX leadership: the series* (Vol. I, pp. 145–82). Greenwich, CT: Information Age.

Graen, G. B. & Uhl-Bien, M. (1995). Relationship-based approach to leadership: development of a leader–member exchange (LMX) theory of leadership over 25 years – applying a multi-level multi-domain perspective. *Leadership Quarterly*, 6, 219–47.

Granholm, A. R. (1991). *Handbook of employee termination*. New York: Wiley.

Granovetter, M. (1973). The strength of weak ties. *American Journal of Sociology*, 78, 1360–80.

Greenhaus, J. H. & Beutell, N. J. (1985). Sources of conflict between work and family roles. *Academy of Management Review*, 10, 76–88.

References

Gross, T. S. (1981). Blueprint for a group move. *Personnel Journal*, 60, 546–7.

Harris, M. M. (1989). Reconsidering the employment interview: a review of recent literature and suggestions for future research. *Personnel Psychology*, 42, 691–726.

Haski-Leventhal, D. & Bargal, D. (2008). The volunteer stages and transitions model: organizational socialization of volunteers. *Human Relations*, 61, 67–102.

Hess, J. A. (1993). Assimilating newcomers into an organization: a cultural perspective. *Journal of Applied Communication Research*, 21, 189–210.

Hess, J. A. (2000). Maintaining nonvoluntary relationship with disliked partners: an investigation into the use of distancing behaviors. *Human Communication Research*, 26, 458–88.

Hill, L. A. (2003). *Becoming a manager: how new managers master the challenges of leadership*. Boston, MA: Harvard Business School Press.

Hochschild, A. R. (1983). *The managed heart*. Berkeley, CA: University of California Press.

Hoffner, C. A., Levine, K. J. & Toohey, R. A. (2008). Socialization to work in late adolescence: the role of television and family. *Journal of Broadcasting & Electronic Media*, 52, 282–302.

Hofstede, G. (1997). From fad to management tool. In *Cultures and organizations: software of the mind* (pp. 178–204). New York: McGraw-Hill.

Holder, T. (1996). Women in nontraditional occupations: information-seeking during organizational entry. *Journal of Business Communication*, 33, 9–26.

Hooghe, M. (2003). Participation in voluntary associations and value indicators: the effect of current and previous participation experiences. *Nonprofit and Voluntary Sector Quarterly*, 32, 47–69.

Hutchinson, K. L. & Brefka, D. S. (1997). Personnel administrators' preferences for résumé content: ten years after. *Journal of Business Communication*, 60, 67–75.

Hylmo, A. (2006). Telecommuting and the contestability of choice: employee strategies to legitimized personal decisions to work in a preferred location. *Management Communication Quarterly*, 19, 541–69.

Hylmo, A. & Buzzanell, P. M. (2002). Telecommuting as viewed through cultural lenses: an empirical investigation of the discourses of utopia, identity, and mystery. *Communication Monographs*, 69, 329–56.

Ibarra, H. (1995). Race, opportunity, and diversity of social circles in managerial networks. *Academy of Management Journal*, 38, 673–703.

Ingersoll, V. H. & Adams, G. B. (1992). The child is "Father" to the manager: images of organizations in US children's literature. *Organization Studies*, 13, 497–519.

Institute of Politics (n.d.). *Women in politics policy report*. Cambridge, MA: Harvard. Available at www.iop.harvard.edu/var/ezp_site/storage/fckeditor/file/policy%20group%20-%20women%20in%20politics%20report.pdf. Accessed February 6, 2009.

References

Jablin, F. M. (1979). Superior–subordinate communication: the state of the art. *Psychological Bulletin*, 86, 1201–22.

Jablin, F. M. (1984). Organizatinal communication: an assimilation approach. In R. N. Bostrom (ed.), *Communication yearbook 8* (pp. 594–626). Beverly Hills, CA: Sage.

Jablin, F. M. (1985). An exploratory study of vocational organizational communication socialization. *Southern Speech Communication Journal*, 50, 261–82.

Jablin, F. M. (1987). Organizational entry, assimilation, and exit. In F. M. Jablin, L. L. Putnam, K. H. Roberts, & L. W. Porter (eds.), *Handbook of organizational communication: an interdisciplinary perspective* (pp. 679–740). Newbury Park, CA: Sage.

Jablin, F. M. (2001). Organizational entry, assimilation, and disengagement/exit. In F. M. Jablin & L. L. Putnam (eds.), *The new handbook of organizational communication: advances in theory, research, and methods* (pp. 732–818). Thousand Oaks, CA: Sage.

Jobstar.com (2009). Available at: http://jobstar.org. Accessed February 12, 2009.

Jobweb.com. (2009). Available at: www.jobweb.com. Accessed February 12, 2009.

Johnson, J. R., Bernhagen, M. J., Miller, V. & Allen, M. (1996). The role of communication in managing reductions in work force. *Journal of Applied Communication Research*, 24, 139–64.

Jones, G. R. (1986). Socialization tactics, self-efficacy, and newcomers' adjustments to organizations. *Academy of Management Journal*, 29, 262–79.

Judge, T. A., Cable, D. M. & Higgins, C. A. (2000). The employment interview: a review of recent research and recommendations for future research. *Human Resource Management Review*, 10, 383–406.

Katz, D. & Kahn, R. L. (1978). *The social psychology of organizations*. New York: John Wiley.

Kirby, E. L. & Krone, K. J. (2002). "The policy exists but you can't really use it." *Journal of Applied Communication Research*, 30, 50–77.

Klatzke, S. R. (2008). Communication and sensemaking during the exit phase of socialization. Unpublished dissertation at the University of Missouri.

Knapp, M. L. & Vangelisti, A. L. (2008). *Interpersonal communication and human relationships* (6th edn.). Boston: Allyn & Bacon

Knouse, S. B. (1994). Impressions of the resume: the effects of applicant education, experience, and impression management. *Journal of Business and Psychology*, 9, 33–45.

Krajewski, H. T., Goffin, R. D., McCarthy, J. M., Rothstein, M. G. & Johnson, N. (2006). Comparing the validity of structured interviews for managerial-level employees: should we look to the past or focus on the future? *Journal of Occupational and Organizational Psychology*, 79, 411–32.

Kram, K. E. (1983). Phases of the mentor relationship. *Academy of Management Journal*, 26, 608–25.

References

Kram, K. E. & Isabella, L. A. (1985). Mentoring alternatives: the role of peer relationships in career development. *Academy of Management Journal*, 28, 110–32.

Kramer, M. W. (1989). Communication during intraorganizational job transfers. *Management Communication Quarterly*, 3, 219–48.

Kramer, M. W. (1993a). Communication after job transfers: social exchange processes in learning new roles. *Human Communication Research*, 20, 147–74.

Kramer, M. W. (1993b). Communication and uncertainty reduction during job transfers: leaving and joining processes. *Communication Monographs*, 60, 178–98.

Kramer, M. W. (1995). A longitudinal study of superior–subordinate communication during job transfers. *Human Communication Research*, 22, 39–64.

Kramer, M. W. (1996). A longitudinal study of peer communication during job transfers: the impact of frequency, quality, and network multiplexity on adjustment. *Human Communication Research*, 23, 59–86.

Kramer, M. W. (2002). Communication in a community theater group: managing multiple group roles. *Communication Studies*, 53, 151–70.

Kramer, M. W. (2004). *Managing uncertainty in organizational communication.* Mahwah, NJ: Lawrence Erlbaum.

Kramer, M. W. (2005). Communication and social exchange processes in community theater groups. *Journal of Applied Communication Research*, 33, 159–82.

Kramer, M. W. (forthcoming). A study of voluntary organizational membership: the assimilation process in a community choir. *Western Journal of Communication*, 74.

Kramer, M. W. & Berman, J. E. (2001). Making sense of a university's culture: an examination of undergraduate students' stories. *Southern Communication Journal*, 66, 297–311.

Kramer, M. W., Dougherty, D. S. & Pierce, T. A. (2004). Communication during a corporate merger: a case of managing uncertainty during organizational change. *Human Communication Research*, 30, 71–101.

Kramer, M. W. & Hess, J. A. (2002). Communication rules for the display of emotions in organizational settings. *Management Communication Quarterly*, 16, 66–80.

Kramer, M.W. & Miller, V. D. (1999). A response to criticisms of socialization research: in support of contemporary conceptualizations of assimilation. *Communication Monographs*, 66, 358–67.

Kramer, M. W. & Noland, T. L. (1999). Communication during job promotions: a case of ongoing assimilation. *Journal of Applied Communication Research*, 27, 335–55.

Kramer, M. W. & Tan, C. L. (2006). Emotion management in dealing with difficult people. In J. M. H. Fritz & B. L. Omdahl (eds.), *Communicating in the workplace with difficult others* (pp. 153–78). New York: Peter Lang.

References

Kramer, M. W. & Walker, M. R. (1998, November). Explorations of vocational socialization through the "real job" colloquialism. Competitive paper presented at the National Communication Association convention in New York.

Langellier, K.M. & Peterson, E. E. (2006). "Somebody's got to pick eggs": family storytelling about work. *Communication Monographs*, 73, 468–73.

Larkey, L. K. (1996). Toward a theory of communicative interactions in culturally diverse workgroups. *Academy of Management Review*, 21, 463–91.

Lee, T. W., Mitchell, T. R., Wise, L. & Fireman, S. (1996). An unfolding model of voluntary employee turnover. *Academy of Management Journal*, 39, 5–36.

Levine, K. J. & Hoffner, C. A. (2006). Adolescents' conceptions of work: what is learned from different sources during anticipatory socialization? *Journal of Adolescent Research*, 21, 647–69.

Lichter, S. R., Lichter, L. S. & Amundson, D. (1997). Does Hollywood hate business or money? *Journal of Communication*, 47, 68–84.

Louis, M. R. (1980). Surprise and sense making: what newcomers experience in entering unfamiliar organizational settings. *Administrative Science Quarterly*, 25, 226–51.

Louis, M. R. (1982). Managing career transitions: a missing link in career development. *Organizational Dynamics*, 10, 68–77.

Louis, M. R., Posner, B. Z. & Powell, G. N. (1983). The availability and helpfulness of socialization practices. *Organizational Dynamics*, 10, 68–77.

Lucas, K. & Buzzanell, P. M. (2004). Blue-collar work, career, and success: occupational narratives of Sisu. *Journal of Applied Communication Research*, 32, 273–92.

Lutgen-Sandvik, P. (2006). Take this job and . . .: quitting and other forms of resistance to workplace bullying. *Communication Monographs*, 73, 406–33.

Martin, J. (1992). *Cultures in organizations: three perspectives*. New York: Oxford University Press.

Martin, J., Feldman, M., Hatch, M. J. & Sitkin, S. B. (1983). The uniqueness paradox in organizational stories. *Administrative Science Quarterly*, 28, 438–53.

McComb, M. (1995). Becoming a travelers' aid volunteer: communication in socialization and training. *Communication Studies*, 46, 297–316.

McGregor, D. M. (1960). *The human side of enterprise*. New York: McGraw-Hill.

McLaughlin, M. L. & Cheatham, T. R. (1977). Effects of communication isolation on job satisfaction of bank tellers: a research note. *Human Communication Research*, 3, 171–5.

Meglino, B. M., DeNisi, A. S., Youngblood, S. A. & Williams, K. J. (1988). Effects of realistic job previews: a comparison using an enhancement and a reduction preview. *Journal of Applied Psychology*, 73, 259–66.

References

Meiner, E. B. & Miller, V. D. (2004). The effect of formality and relational tone on supervisor/subordinate negotiation episodes. *Western Journal of Communication*, 68, 302–21.

Mendenhall, M. & Oddou, G. (1985). The dimensions of expatriate acculturation: a review. *Academy of Management Review*, 10, 39–47.

Mignerey, J. T., Rubin, R. B. & Gorden, W. I. (1995). Organizational entry: an investigation of newcomer communication behavior and uncertainty. *Communication Research*, 22, 54–85.

Miller, K. I., Considine, J. & Garner, J. (2007). "Let me tell you about my job": exploring the terrain of emotion in the workplace. *Management Communication Quarterly*, 20, 231–60.

Miller, V. D. & Buzzanell, P. M. (1996). Toward a research agenda for the second employment interview. *Journal of Applied Communication Research*, 24, 165–80.

Miller, V. D. & Jablin, F. M. (1991). Information seeking during organization entry: influences, tactics, and a model of the process. *Academy of Management Review*, 16, 92–120.

Miller, V. D., Jablin, F. M., Casey, M. K., Lamphear-Van Horn, M. & Ethington, C. (1996). The maternity leave as role negotiation process. *Journal of Management Issues*, 8, 286–309.

Monge, P. R. & Contractor, N. S. (2001). Emergence of communication networks. In F. M. Jablin & L. L. Putnam (eds.), *The new handbook of organizational communication: advances in theory, research, and methods* (pp. 440–502). Thousand Oaks, CA: Sage.

Moreland, R. L. & Levine, J. M. (2001). Socialization in organizations and work groups. In M. E. Turner (ed.), *groups at work: theory and research* (pp. 69–112). Mahwah, NJ: Lawrence Erlbaum.

Morrison, E. W. (1993a). Longitudinal study of the effects of information seeking on newcomer socialization. *Journal of Applied Psychology*, 78, 173–83.

Morrison, E. W. (1993b). Newcomer information seeking: exploring types, modes, sources, and outcomes. *Academy of Management Journal*, 36, 557–89.

Morrison, E. W. (1995). Information usefulness and acquisition during organizational encounter. *Management Communication Quarterly*, 9, 131–55.

MOW International Research Team (1987). *The meaning of working*. New York: Academic Press.

Muchinsky, P. M. & Harris, S. L. (1977). The effect of applicant sex and scholastic standing on the evaluation of job applicant resumes in sex-typed occupations. *Journal of Vocational Behavior*, 11, 95–107.

Mumby, D. K. (1987). The political function of narrative in organizations. *Communication Monographs*, 54, 113–27.

Myers, K. K. (2005). A burning desire: assimilation into a fire department. *Management Communication Quarterly*, 18, 344–84.

Myers, K. K. & Oetzel, J. G. (2003). Exploring the dimensions of organizational assimilation: creating and validating a measure. *Communication Quarterly*, 51, 438–57.

Napier, N. K., Simmons, G. & Stratton, K. (1989). Communication during a merger: the experience of two banks. *Human Resource Planning*, 12, 105–22.

Nathanson, A. I., Wilson, B. J., McGee, J. & Sebastian, M. (2002). Counteracting the effects of female stereotypes on television via active mediation. *Journal of Communication*, 52, 922–37.

Nelson, D. L. & Quick, J. C. (1991). Social support and newcomer adjustment in organizations: Attachment theory at work. *Journal of Organizational Behavior*, 12, 543–54.

Oliphant, V. N. & Alexander, E. R., III (1982). Reactions to resumes as a function of determinateness, applicant characteristics, and sex of raters. *Personnel Psychology*, 35, 829–42.

O'Reilly, C. A. & Roberts, K. H. (1977). Task group structure, communication and effectiveness in three organizations. *Journal of Applied Psychology*, 62, 674–81.

Ostroff, C. & Kozlowski, S. W. J. (1992). Organizational socialization as a learning process: the role of information acquisition. *Personnel Psychology*, 45, 849–74.

Our stories: communication professionals' narratives of sexual harassment (1992). *Journal of Applied Communication Research*, 20, 363–90.

Pacanowsky, M. E. & O'Donnell-Truijillo, N. (1983). Organizational communication as cultural performance. *Communication Monographs*, 50, 126–47.

Peter, L. J. & Hull, R. (1969). *The Peter Principle: why things always go wrong.* New York: William Morrow.

Peterson, G. L. (2000). Part b. Microsoft revisited. In G. L. Peterson (ed.), *Communicating in organizations: a casebook* (pp. 26–31). Boston: Allyn and Bacon.

Peterson, G. W. & Peters, D. F. (1983). Adolescents' construction of social reality: the impact of television and peers. *Youth and Society*, 15, 67–85.

Pierce, T. & Dougherty, D. S. (2002). The construction, enactment, and maintenance of power-as-domination through an acquisition. *Management Communication Quarterly*, 16, 129–64.

Planalp, S. (2003). The unacknowledged role of emotion in theories of close relationship: how do theories feel? *Communication Theory*, 13, 78–99.

Poole, M. S., Seibold, D. R. & McPhee, R.D. (1985). Group decision-making as a structuration process. *Quarterly Journal of Speech*, 71, 74–102.

Porter, L. W. Lawler, E. E. & Hackman, J. R. (1975) *Behavior in organizations.* New York: McGraw-Hill.

Postmes, T., Tanis, M. & de Wit, B. (2001). Communication and commitment in organizations: a social identity approach. *Group Processes & Intergroup Relations*, 4, 227–46.

References

Premack, S. L. & Wanous, J. P. (1985). A meta-analysis of realistic job review experiments. *Journal of Applied Psychology*, 73, 706–19.

Putnam, L. L. & Poole, M. S. (1987). Conflict and negotiation. In F. M. Jablin, L. L. Putnam, K. H. Roberts, & L. W. Porter (eds.), *Handbook of organizational communication* (pp. 549–99). Newbury Park, CA: Sage.

Putnam, L. L. & Stohl, C. (1996). Bona fide groups: an alternative perspective for communication and small group decision making. In R. Y. Hirokawa & M. S. Poole (eds.), *Communication and group decision making* (2nd edn.) (pp. 147–78). Thousand Oaks, CA: Sage.

Quinn, R. E. & Cameron, K. (1983). Organizational life cycles and shifting criteria of effectiveness: some preliminary evidence. *Management Science*, 29, 33–51.

Ragins, B. R. & Cotton, J. L. (1999). Mentor functions and outcomes: a comparison of men and women in formal and informal mentoring relationships. *Journal of Applied Psychology*, 84, 529–50.

Ralston, S. M. & Kirkwood, W. G. (1995). Overcoming managerial bias in employment interviewing. *Journal of Applied Communication Research*, 23, 75–92.

Reutter, L., Field, P. A. & Campbell, I. E. (1997). Socialization into nursing: nursing students as learners. *Journal of Nursing Education*, 36, 149–55.

Rodgers, W. (1969). *Think: a biography of the Watsons and IBM*. New York: Stern & Day.

Roethlisberger, F. J. (1941). The Hawthorne experiments. In *Management and Morale*. Cambridge, MA: Harvard University Press.

Roloff, M. E. (1981). Social exchange: key concepts. In *Interpersonal communication* (pp. 13–32). Beverly Hills, CA: Sage.

Rosenfeld, L. B., Richman, J. M. & May, S. K. (2004). Information adequacy, job satisfaction and organizational culture in a dispersed-network organization. *Journal of Applied Communication Research*, 32, 28–54.

Rosner, B., Halcrow, A. & Levins, A. (2003, April 16). *How to protect yourself from claims that employees were forced to quit*. Available at http://abcnews.go.com/sections/business/CornerOffice/CORNEROFFICE.html. Found May 1, 2003.

Rotondo, D. M. & Perrewe, P. L. (2000). Coping with career plateau: an empirical examination of what works and what doesn't. *Journal of Applied Social Psychology*, 30, 2622–46.

Rusbult, C. E. & Zembrodt, I. M. (1983). Responses to dissatisfaction in romantic involvements: a multidimensional scaling analysis. *Journal of Experimental Social Psychology*, 19, 274–93.

Ryan, A. M. & Tippins, N. T. (2004). Attracting and selecting: what psychological research tells us. *Human Resource Management*, 43, 305–18.

Schein, E. H. (1968). Organizational socialization and the profession of management. *Industrial Management Review*, 9, 1–16.

Schlossberg, N. K. (1981). A model for analyzing human adaptation to transition. *The Counseling Psychologist*, 9, 2–18.

Schweiger, D. M. & DeNisi, A. S. (1991). Communication with employees following a merger: a longitudinal field experiment. *Academy of Management Journal*, 34, 110–35.

Scott, C. & Myers, K. K. (2005). The socialization of emotion: learning emotion management at the fire station. *Journal of Applied Communication Research*, 33, 67–92.

Scott, C. R. (2007). Communication and social identity theory: existing and potential connections in organizational identification research. *Communication Studies*, 58, 123–38.

Scott, C. R., Connaughton, S. L., Diaz-Saenz, H. R. et al. (1999). The impacts of communication and multiple identifications on intent to leave: a multimethodological exploration. *Management Communication Quarterly*, 12, 400–35.

Shen, W. & Cannella, A. A., Jr. (2002). Revisiting the performance consequences of CEO succession: the impacts of successor type, postsuccession senior executive turnover, and departing CEO tenure. *Academy of Management Journal*, 45, 717–33.

Shuler, S. & Sypher, B. D. (2000). Seeking emotional labor: when managing the heart enhances the work experience. *Management Communication Quarterly*, 14, 50–89.

Sias, P. M. & Cahill, D. J. (1998). From coworkers to friends: the development of peer friendships in the workplace. *Western Journal of Communication*, 62, 273–99.

Sias, P. M. & Jablin, F. M. (1995). Differential superior–subordinate relations, perceptions of fairness, and coworker communication. *Human Communication Research*, 22, 5–38.

Sias, P.M., Kramer, M.W. & Jenkins, E. (1997). A comparison of the communication behaviors of temporary employees and new hires. *Communication Research*, 24, 731–54.

Signorielli, N. & Kahlenberg, S. (2001). Television's world of work in the nineties. *Journal of Broadcasting and Electronic Media*, 45, 4–22.

Smith, R. (2007, February 14). Crime scene investigators. *Nature*, 445, 794.

Smith, R. C. & Eisenberg, E. M. (1987). Conflict at Disneyland: a root-metaphor analysis. *Communication Monographs*, 54, 367–80.

Smith, R. C. & Turner, P. K. (1995). A social constructionist reconfiguration of metaphor analysis: an application of "SCMA" to organizational socialization theorizing. *Communication Monographs*, 62, 152–81.

Stohl, C. (1986). The role of memorable messages in the process of organizational socialization. *Communication Quarterly*, 34, 231–49.

Tan, C. L. (2008). The communication and management of career change: a study of individuals' experiences of the social process of voluntary downward career change in Singapore. Unpublished dissertation at the University of Missouri.

Taylor, F. W. (1911). *The principles of scientific management*. New York: Harper.

Teboul, J. C. B. (1994). Facing and coping with uncertainty during organizational encounters. *Management Communication Quarterly*, 8, 190–224.

Terkanian, D. (2006). Lifetime "career" changes. *Occupational Outlook Quarterly* (online), 50 Available at (2). www.bls.gov/opub/ooq/2006/summer/grabbag.htm#C. Accessed September 28, 2009.

Thibaut, J. W. & Kelley, H. H. (1959). *The social psychology of groups*. New York: John Wiley.

Thoms, P., McMasters, R., Roberts, M. R. & Dombkowski, D. A. (1999). Resume characteristics as predictors of an invitation to interview. *Journal of Business and Psychology*, 13, 339–56.

Tourish, D., Paulsen, N., Hobman, E. & Bordia, P. (2004). The downsides of downsizing: communication processes and information needs in the aftermath of a workforce reduction strategy. *Management Communication Quarterly*, 17, 485–516.

Tremblay, M., Roger, A. & Toulouse, J. M. (1995). Career plateau and work attitudes: an empirical study of managers. *Human Relations*, 48, 221–37.

Tushman, M. L. (1977a). A political approach to organizations: a review and rationale. *Academy of Management Review*, 2, 206–16.

Tushman, M. L. (1977b). Special boundary roles in the innovation process. *Administrative Science Quarterly*, 22, 587–605.

United States Department of Labor (2005, April 28). *Employment of high school students rises by grade*. Available at www.bls.gov/opub/ted/2005/apr/wk4/art04.htm. Accessed February 4, 2009.

US Equal Employment Opportunity Commission (2004, September 4). *Discrimination practices*. Available at www.eeoc.gov/abouteeo/overview_practices.html. Accessed February 16, 2009.

US Equal Employment Opportunity Commission (2008, March 11). *Sexual harassment*. Available at www.eeoc.gov/types/sexual_harassment.html. Accessed March 18, 2009.

Van Maanen, J. (1975). Breaking in: socialization to work. In R. Dubin (ed.), *Handbook of work, organization, and society* (pp. 67–120). Chicago: Rand McNally.

Van Maanen, J. & Kunda, G. (1989). "Real feelings": emotional expression and organizational culture. *Research in Organizational Behavior*, 11, 43–103.

Van Maanen, J. & Schein, E. G. (1979). Toward a theory of organizational socialization. In B. M. Staw (ed.), *Research in organizational behavior* (pp. 209–64). Greenwich, CT: JAI Press, Inc.

Waldeck, J. H. & Myers, K. K. (2008). Organizational assimilation theory, research, and implications for multiple areas of the discipline: a state of the art review. In C. S. Beck (ed.), *Communication yearbook 31* (pp. 322–67). New York: Lawrence Erlbaum.

Waldeck, J. H., Seibold, D. R. & Flanagin, A. J. (2004). Organizational assimilation and communication technology use. *Communication Monographs, 71,* 161–83.

Wanous, J. P., Poland, T. D., Premack, S. L. & Davis, K. S. (1992). The effects of met expectations on newcomer attitudes and behaviors: a review and meta-analysis. *Journal of Applied Psychology, 77,* 288–97.

Watson, W. E., Kumar, K. & Michaelsen, L. K. (1993). Cultural diversity's impact on interaction process and performance: comparing homogeneous and diverse task groups. *Academy of Management Journal, 36,* 590–602.

Weber, M. (1947). *The theory of social and economic organizations.* Trans. A. M. Henderson & T. Parsons. Ed. T. Parsons, New York: Oxford University Press.

Weick, K. E. (1995). *Sensemaking in organizations.* Thousand Oaks, CA: Sage.

Weick, K. E. (2001). *Making sense of the organization.* Malden, MA: Blackwell Publications.

Wiesner, W. H. & Cronshaw, S. F. (1988). A meta-analytic investigation of the impact of interview format and degree of structure on the validity of the employment interview. *Journal of Occupational Psychology, 61,* 275–90.

Wilson, C. E. (1983). Toward understanding the process of organizational leave-taking. Paper presented at the annual meeting of the Speech Communication Association, Washington, DC.

Wood, J. T. (1992). Tell our stories: narratives as a basis for theorizing sexual harassment. *Journal of Applied Communication, 20,* 349–62.

Yate, M. (2008). Knock 'em dead 2009: the ultimate job search guide. Avon, MA: Adams Publishing.

Zhu, Y., May, S. K. & Rosenfeld, L. B. (2004). Information adequacy and job satisfaction during merger and acquisition. *Management Communication Quarterly, 18,* 241–70.

Zorn, T. E. & Gregory, K. W. (2005). Learning the ropes together: assimilation and friendship development among first-year male medical students. *Health Communication, 17,* 211–31.

Index

Numbers in italics indicate entries in the References section.

212

Index